Herencia
COOKBOOK

Herencia
COOKBOOK

Celebrating and honoring
SalviMex culture and matriarchs through food

Written by: Bernadette Molina
Chief Recipe Consultants:
Rose Ortega and Sandra Molina

ROSETTE
PUBLICATIONS

Text, design and photography copyright 2020 by Rosette Publications

Publisher's Cataloging-in-Publication Data
Names: Molina, Bernadette, author.
Title: Herencia cookbook / written by Bernadette Molina.
Description: Downey, CA: Rosette Publications, 2020.
Identifiers: LCCN: 2020915812 | ISBN: 978-1-7355065-0-0 (pbk.) | 978-1-7355065-1-7 (ebook)
Subjects: LCSH Cooking, Mexican. | Mexican American cooking. | Cooking--El Salvador. |
Cooking, Latin American. | Cooking--Central America. | Hispanic Americans--Food. | Hispanic
Americans--Ethnic identity. | Hispanic Americans--Social life and customs. | BISAC COOKING / Regional & Ethnic / Latin
American | COOKING / Regional & Ethnic / Central American & South American | COOKING / Regional & Ethnic / Mexican
Classification: LCC TX716.A1 M 2020 | DDC 641.59728--dc23
Printed in the United States of America
Proofread by M. Guillermina Bagilet and Gabriella Alderman
Designed by Miguel Martínez
Photography by Ezekiel Barrera and Eric Gomez

ACKNOWLEDGMENTS

First and foremost, I would like to thank my husband, who has been the biggest supporter of this book from the very first moment back when it was just an aspiration in my heart. My husband is Salvadorian-American, and has helped me get deeper in touch with my Salvi roots. For this, I am so thankful.

I would also like to thank my son, who is my biggest motivator. I wrote and published this book while I was pregnant with him. I put everything into this book. I did it for him, so that he would be born into a world with positive Salvadorian-American and Mexican-American representation. And I hope he will be proud that his mother contributed, in a small way, to improve our cultural representation.

I would like to thank my father, who is Mexican-American, and took me with him on his frequent travels back to his native land. On our road trips to Sonora, Mexico, and every day in life, he taught me to be proud of my roots. He was raised by strong women and reminded me of my own power, always. Above all, my father showed me pure and unconditional love. If everyone had a father like him, the world would truly be a better place.

There are so many women who influenced me to become the woman I am today and who, therefore, influenced this book. Above all, mi madre querida, my dear mother Rose. I am married and, as I write this, I am pregnant with my first child, and I find myself needing my mother now more than ever. There is so much of her I admire.

I long to be like her in so many ways. When she still lived in El Salvador, she graduated from high school and, later, vocational school. Then, she moved to Los Angeles to start her adult life. In Los Angeles, she met my father and they built their life together.

When I was growing up, I watched in awe as she balanced entrepreneurship, motherhood, marriage, and social life, all while wearing Estée Lauder perfume and lipstick. More than anyone, my mother taught me that I could have it all if I really wanted it and worked hard for it. She still reminds me to pull strength from deep down inside, and to pray for my path to be illuminated whenever I feel uncertain.

Influenced by my father's Mexican culture, my mother started her own Mexican bakery when I was growing up. She managed to cook her own traditional Salvadorian recipes and my father's favorite Mexican recipes at home, all while running a business! And, through her cooking, I received the best gift: all my cultures served together, harmoniously, and warm, on my dinner plate! Mama Rose is gifted at many things, and cooking is just one of her many gifts or dones.

Besides being blessed with a beautiful, hard-working and gifted mother, there are other women who influenced and molded me. Most specially, my two Nanas who were a big part of my formative years.

My Nana Isabel, my father's mother, filled my stomach and heart with her delicious Mexican cooking since I was a little girl. Her home in Los Angeles felt like Sonora, Mexico. I feel her love for me is and was so pure, it transcends time and generations. Sadly, she passed away one month before my eighteenth birthday. I am now thirty, and I still think of her almost every single day. I feel her spirit guiding me to be the best mujer I can be.

I also recall my Nana Lupita, my great-grandmother, who was my Nana Isabel's mother. I had the privilege of knowing my Nana Lupita for the first ten years of my life. I remember her with her hair styled in finger waves—she loved that style! Those finger waves gleamed as white as the snow that fell in that mountain town in Sonora, where she lived and where my father was raised. When my family and I would visit her and spend the night, my Nana Lupita would pray with me in Spanish. I believe her prayers still shield me to this day.

I would also like to say that this book could not exist without my suegra. Let me tell you something, the best part about getting married, for me, was inheriting a second family. My suegra is like a second mother to me, and spoils me as such. This has been especially true lately, during the course of my pregnancy. She showers me with affection (and snacks!) and we have grown closer than ever. It swells my heart to think about how much she helped me with this book as well. I wish everyone had a suegra like her!

Finally, a big shout out to my cuñadas, tías, primas, hermanas, amigas, comadres, and so many more women and people in my life who inspired me to create Herencia Cookbook!

ÁRBOL DE FAMILIA

Honoring our culture and the matriarchs who nourished us.

My Salvadorian roots from my mother's side, my Mexican roots from my father's side, and my Los Angeles upbringing molded me into who I am today. This identity is what I inherited from my parents. It is my herencia. This identity inspired me to write Herencia Cookbook and honor my Latinidad through recipes and memories. After all, my Latinidad is the best herencia my parents could have ever given me.

In addition to honoring my culture, I wish to honor the matriarchs who nourished me. How many of us have a tía who is an amazing home cook? Or dream of perfecting abuelita's recipes? My goal is to elevate the home cooks we love and celebrate their recipes, cooking techniques, and heritage.

When I moved out of my parents' home and into my own place for the first time, I felt like I joined a support network of women who were all willing to swap recipes and offer tips to help me improve my cooking. Even the memories of my Nana's cooking came back to me, as I remembered to add un poquito de esto y otra pizca de aquello, just like she did. (I also desperately called my mom more times than I am willing to admit.)This book is for them. It is an homage to the matriarchs who feed, nourish, and nurture us. They guide us and teach us. They show us love in so many different ways, and so often it is through food

AUTHENTIC FLAVOR WITH A MODERN TWIST

I want this book to make cooking more accessible. Many of us have a lot of things to balance. After all, if you are Latinx-American, like me, you are already balancing dual identities and so much more. Perhaps you balance a full-time job, a side hustle, a relationship, caring for your children, your parents, your siblings, and yourself (mind, body, and spirit). With all those responsibilities, why not take some shortcuts in the kitchen? (I can hear the abuelitas gasping now.) But yes, it is OK to take some practical shortcuts in the kitchen.

I personally refuse to feel guilty about implementing modern kitchen hacks when I cook. It won't make my Latin dishes any less authentic! I tell myself: hey, I'm Latin, I made it, and I like it. That is all the authenticity I need! Why use a molcajete when I can use a blender? Why chop things by hand when I can use my food processor? My dishwasher is not meant to serve as extra storage space; it's meant to help me out so I don't have to wash the dishes by hand! Because, hey, my hands are tired after working on a computer all day.

In addition to cooking authentic foods with modern hacks, I also want to take the intimidation out of cooking. There is no need to be intimidated in the kitchen! Remember, patience and guidance goes a long way in the kitchen and in life.

I also want to say: I am the author of a cookbook, but I am not a professional chef. I taught myself and learned from the master home cooks in my life—my mom, my Nanas, and my suegra—who have made some of the most delicious food I have ever tasted. Yet, these señoras did not go to culinary arts school. They are not professional chefs. Rather, they are talented and gifted home cooks who taught me to follow my intuition in the kitchen, remain ever-present while cooking, and be intentional with every ingredient.

Think of some of those complicated dishes that so beautifully define our culture. Who made them for you? It was probably made by a señora who loved you so much. These señoras learned by doing, and so did I. If I can write a cookbook based on their recipes and mine, then I promise, you can get down in the kitchen too! This book is here to provide you with delicious recipes and some tips to make cooking them a bit easier.

MAKING CLASSIC
RECIPES A BIT HEALTHIER
WITHOUT COMPROMISING FLAVOR

In addition to offering tips on how to make cooking more practical and accessible for the modern home cook, this book also offers tips on how to make some of the traditional foods we love so much, in the most nutritious way we can. If you are like me, then perhaps you have a large family that you care about deeply. Maybe you have an abuelita with diabetes. Maybe your father has high blood pressure. Perhaps your mother has high cholesterol. These diseases are all too common in our families. Of course, this book is not meant to diagnose or treat these diseases. Rather, it offers you the opportunity to make the most nutritious choices from the traditional classic foods you love and may have grown up eating.

As you look through the book, you will see that I offer easy-to-follow tips to make nutritious recipes. At home, I strive to make healthy choices without compromising flavor, and I will be sharing my secrets with you. For example, I may enjoy my enchiladas with salad instead of rice and beans or double check that I have all food groups on my plate. Other times, I mindfully indulge in a delicious treat and savor every bite. (Because, hey, balance!) I am not a nutritionist. I am just an everyday woman who wants to make the best choices for her life. My goal here is to find a right balance for my life, and I hope my tips to achieve this can offer you some value as well.

MI JEFECITA MONCHI BERNADETTE EL WILLY

Mi Herencia: Honoring Our Culture and Matriarchs through Food, While Offering Modern and Sometimes Healthy Tips

As you can see by now, this book embodies many different identities, just like I do. I am a mujer. I am a first-generation US born Latina raised in Los Angeles. I am half Mexican-American and half Salvadorian-American. I am an individual with ambitions, dreams, and hobbies. I am also a daughter, a wife, an amiga and, by the time this book is released, a mother. Like most Latinas, I have had to learn how to be as soft as silk and as hard as iron. This duality ensures I offer my best to myself, my husband, my parents, my career, and soon, pues, my first-born child.

I welcome you to join me on this journey of honoring our ancestors through food and memories, via Herencia Cookbook. If you're anything like me, these traditional foods will spark some of the warmest memories. Do you think of your grandma when you eat beans? Do you think of your madrina when you eat flan? Whenever you drink a caldo, do you think of how well your mother took care of you when you were sick? (Or do you, perhaps, ask yourself why your mom would always make caldos on the hottest days of summer?) When you make a recipe that used to be challenging but is now easy, do you recall the sister or homegirl who gave you that special tip that made the whole recipe suddenly make sense? I know I do. Let's look at these recipes together, with as little fuss as possible, remember the señoras of our lives, and make something that's delicious, fun, and good for our bodies!

TABLE OF CONTENTS

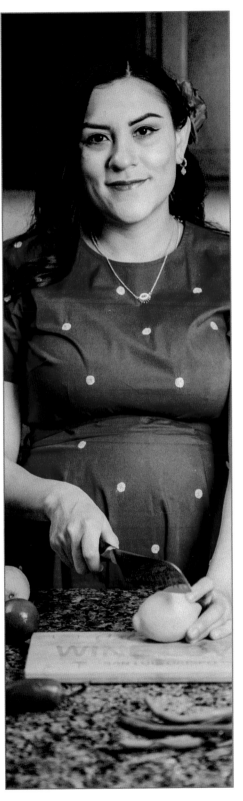

Icon Breakdown

Each recipe includes the following icons to indicate level of difficulty, cooking time, and serving amount.

Difficulty Icons

The difficulty meter ranges from easy to difficult depending on the number of steps needed to prepare and cook each recipe.

Easy | Moderate | Difficult

Cooking Time

The clock icon will display the amount of time needed to prepare and cook each recipe from start to finish.

Fast | Medium | Long

Serves Amount

This icon displays the number of servings, or the number of people each recipe will serve.

SALSAS INTRODUCTION

Salsas are a pillar in my personal cooking style. Can you relate? They can liven up any meal. They are a great way to get more veggies in your diet and they taste great! Before I started writing this book, when it was just an idea in my heart, I knew I had to include a section devoted to salsas.

Growing up, there were always homemade salsas on hand or ingredients to make salsas in the fridge. Those spicy flavors influenced both my palate and how I cook. At my home, today, if you can't find salsas in my fridge, you will at least find tomatoes, peppers, onion, garlic, and cilantro in my garden, because I cook with these ingredients so often!

When my husband and I were first dating, there were a lot of traits I was looking for to determine if we were compatible. One big question I had was: do we both like the same types of food? Do we both like spicy food? Imagine my joy when I made a special salsa just for him and he loved it. In time, I came to the conclusion that if a couple is on the same page with their "spice-comfort level," they are probably compatible. I love spicy, flavorful salsas and could not imagine being married to someone who would not enjoy them with me. And, something tells me, my husband enjoys being married to someone who refuses to cook bland food. After all, he certainly was happy to help me taste test all the recipes in this book! I hope you enjoy these salsas as much as we do.

PICO DE GALLO OR CHIMOL?

I am half Mexican-American on my father's side and half Salvadorian-American on my mother's side. However, my home was primarily influenced by the Mexican side of my family. (I think it is because my dad's family was mostly all in Los Angeles and a lot of my mom's family was still in El Salvador.) When I first met my darling husband, el Willy, as I affectionately call him, we instantly made a connection as we had a lot in common and a lot to talk about. The reason? He's Salvadorian-American as well. As things became serious and I finally had the chance to meet his loving family, I was excited to connect with them because we already had two things in common: el Willy and El Salvador.

One of the first times I visited them, my suegra offered me chimol. Surprised, I smiled, blinked, and nodded, indicating that I accepted her offer. Who was I to despreciar a la señora? Then I leaned over to Willy and asked him, "What the hell is chimol?" He chuckled and whispered back, "It's basically like pico de gallo." Ironically, here I was, ready to brag about my Salvi cred, and yet I had never even heard that word before. Clearly, I had something new to learn.

When I came home later that day, I interrogated mom about it: "What the heck is this and why have you never told me about it? What other marvelous Salvi secrets are you hiding from me, mujer?" She said she knew about chimol but that, while similar, it is a bit different from pico de gallo After she explained, I could understand why. My in-laws prepare chimol with diced tomatoes, white onions, and cilantro leaves: delicious, but missing the kick I was so used to. I was used to my chunky salsas with having tomatoes, red onions, minced cilantro, and minced jalapeño or serrano peppers. Sometimes, when feeling extra creative, I add chopped cucumbers for a refreshing crunch too. (Or, if I am really going all out, I add chopped nopales and the pico de gallo turns into a cactus salad. But I digress.) Now when my in-laws and I have get-togethers, there is typically Salvi chimol, Mexican pico de gallo, and a whole lot of other tasty salsas.

I love pico de gallo so much because it can be the cornerstone of many meals! Put it on top of casamiento and you have a vegan burrito bowl; eat it with a Mexican quesadilla and suddenly you went from having a snack to having a meal. Even if you just eat it with chips, it can feel as satisfying as heaven!

However you like to enjoy it and whatever you decide to call it, this recipe can give you the foundational tips to create your personalized version of chunky tomato salsa every time. Join me!

FAST
Less than 15 minutes.

DIFFICULTY
EASY
¡Facilísimo!

SERVES **4**

Ingredients:

- 3 or 4 roma tomatoes
- 1 medium red onion
- A handful of cilantro
- 1 or 2 lemons
- 1 tablespoon of salt
- 1 small cucumber (or half of a larger one), optional
- 1 or 2 serrano peppers, optional

Directions:

- Rinse the vegetables.
- Dice the tomatoes, onion, and cucumber. You want these three ingredients to be roughly the same size.
- Finely mince the cilantro leaves.
- Put the chopped ingredients together in a bowl.
- Squeeze the lemon all over the vegetables and mix everything. You want the ingredients' flavors to perfectly blend together.
- Sprinkle with salt.
- Optional: finely chop the pepper while the other vegetables' flavors blend together. The smaller the pieces, the better! You don't want big chunks of pepper ruining the flavor; rather, minced pieces will complement this salsa. Take your time to devein the pepper and remove all seeds: this will remove any bitterness.
- Add the minced pepper to the rest of the salsa and stir to combine flavors.

¡BUEN PROVECHO!

Señora Advice

*If you have a food processor, you can cut the tomatoes, cucumber, and onion into fourths and put them into the food processor with the salt and lime. Remove from the food processor and add the minced cilantro and pepper at the end. There is no shame in having the food processor do the chopping for you and ease the process! It's important to take care of our hands.

*Enjoy this delicious salsa with chips as a snack, or on top of tacos as a garnish to your meal. This salsa also pairs well with carne asada and agua fresca at a summer BBQ

ROSA'S SALSA ROJA

I cannot write about salsa roja without thinking of my dear mother. When we would sit together as a family for dinner, there was almost always salsa roja at the table. We would drizzle it on meat, on top of rice, or over veggies. We would even pour it in soups or over our tacos. And we didn't just enjoy her delicious salsa roja at intimate family dinners; my father was known for frequently hosting a lot of family reunions, all of which included my mother's mouth-watering salsas. (Lucky me: my birthday parties were also a place marker/excuse for huge family gatherings.) At these gatherings, each table was decorated with Rose's Salsa Roja, accompanied by chips for guests to snack on while they caught up with each other.

As an adult, I eat this salsa for comfort but also for convenience. The salsa is versatile. It goes with many different dishes as I mentioned above. And its heat level is very easy to customize. For instance, if you are making this salsa for someone who can't handle spice too well, use less chile and more tomatoes. If you are a huge fan of spice, then add more chile to the salsa.

In addition to the versatility of the salsa, there is also beauty in its simplicity. Tomatoes. Peppers. Garlic. Salt. And that's it.

There is no way to mess this one up. It was one of the first things I learned to make from scratch when growing up. I thought to myself, "Wow, ya estoy lista para casarme." Just kidding. I never thought about being ready for marriage as an adolescent. What I thought was, "Wow, I can make something from scratch, and it tastes good. I am on my way to becoming an independent adult who won't starve to death." Or as my mom would say jokingly, "ya puedes sobrevivir," which means, "you can survive by yourself." Thanks, mom.

This salsa is still one of my kitchen staples. I almost always have a batch in my fridge, and it doesn't last long! I love to make it when I am hosting guests. Some people have friends over for wine and charcuterie boards; I invite friends over for tequila and salsa tasting.

FAST
Less than 15 minutes.

DIFFICULTY
EASY
¡Facilísimo!

SERVES
4

Ingredients:

- 2-3 roma tomatoes
- 1 serrano pepper
- 1 garlic clove, peeled
- 1 tablespoon of salt
- 1 teaspoon of olive oil for the pan, optional

Directions:

- Rinse the vegetables.
- On the stove, warm a comal or nonstick pan.
- Once the pan is warm, add the whole tomatoes, garlic clove, and chile pepper.
- Lower the heat and cover the pan. Check on it constantly and, using tongs, turn the ingredients to char them evenly on each side. You should see them start to develop a golden color.
- Once the tomatoes start cracking and leaking juice, and the ingredients start getting mushy, you are ready to make the salsa.
- Remove the stem from the pepper and put all the ingredients into a heat-safe blender with a teaspoon of salt.
- Blend until you have the desired consistency.

¡BUEN PROVECHO!

BERNIE'S SALSA VERDE

FAST
Less than 15 minutes.

DIFFICULTY
EASY
¡Facilísimo!

SERVES
4

I love all kinds of salsas, but my all-time favorite salsa is salsa verde, which is also known as tomatillo salsa. It adds so much flavor to dishes! It is just the right amount of spicy without overpowering a dish. It is tangy and makes my lips pucker: I can put it on a taco, in a burrito bowl, in my caldo, or just eat it with chips. It compliments almost everything, and I never get tired of it.

The stars of the show in this salsa are the tomatillos themselves. When shopping for them, make sure they are plump, but not too hard and not soggy either. After peeling and washing the tomatillos, I roast them on the comal to bring out the flavor. I love seeing them dance as I prepare the other ingredients. I also feel like a badass when I'm able to roast a chile on a comal without coughing.

So, how is it done? It couldn't be easier! I throw in the tomatillos, pepper, cilantro, salt, and fresh lemon juice in the blender. Once it has a nice liquid consistency, I pour it into a bowl and garnish with freshly diced white onion. It is so quick to make and so delicious.

I love to presumir a mis invitados (show off to my guests) that I made my own tomatillo salsa. Of course, it is easier and faster to buy it at the carniceria and it will taste good. But, somehow, it is just much more satisfying to make the salsa at home with fresh ingredients (preferably organic) and an extra pinch of love! Read on for the recipe on how to make this salsa at home, in a quick and easy way.

Ingredients:

- 3-4 large tomatillos
- 1 or 2 serrano peppers
- 1 handful of cilantro
- 2 or 3 limes
- 1/2 medium to large white onion
- 1 tablespoon salt

Directions:

- Warm a comal to medium to low heat.
- Rinse the vegetables.
- Once warm, put the whole tomatillos and peppers on the comal.
- Use tongs to turn them as needed so they are browned/charred on each side evenly.
- While the tomatillos and peppers cook on the comal, chop the onion and set it to the side. No need to cook this one!
- Once they are evenly cooked, the skin of the tomatillos will start to crack and seep out juice, which means it's ready!
- Put the tomatillos, chile (without stem), lime juice, salt, and fresh cilantro into a heat-safe blender and liquefy.
- Pour the salsa into a bowl and add the chopped onions. Stir.

¡BUEN PROVECHO!

MIXED SALSA, DOS GENERACIONES

OK, so now that you've learned about how to make red and green salsas, you are ready for the next story. As I was writing this book, I consulted my mom often (so much that I've credited as chief consultant of this book). When I told her about the salsas, she said to me, "mija, you have salsa roja and salsa verde—but how could you forget about our special mixed salsa?" You see, my mom sometimes can't decide between red salsa or green salsa, so she sort of mixes both together. By doing this, she gets the deep flavors of red salsa, the tanginess of green salsa, and the spiciness that they both offer, combined.

I loved her idea of including the mixed salsa in this book. It's sort of a combination of her favorite red salsa and my favorite green salsa, so how could I not include it? After all, my mother is the woman who taught me how to cook! Without her cooking skills and gifts, I would not be the confident home cook I am today. I grew up tasting her food and watching her cook. Of course, this influenced my own skills in the kitchen! Entonces, without la Mera Mera's guidance over the years, pues, there would be no cookbook!

This salsa is a great example of how my mom's and my own cooking styles often come together when we collaborate in the kitchen, and, of course, in many other aspects of life. Therefore, this recipe is especially dedicated to my jefecita, as an ode to how her influence molded me into the woman I am today. Her example and advice shaped so many aspects of my personality. From balancing work and family life to multitasking in the kitchen with ease, and never leaving the house without lipstick, perfume, and a winged liner (OK, the last one I discovered for myself), my mom deeply influenced who I am and how I use cooking as a way to strengthen my intuition and sense of self.

We are still talking about food, right? OK pues, let's get started with this yummy salsa.

FAST
Less than
15 minutes.

**DIFFICULTY
EASY**
¡Facilísimo!

SERVES 4

Ingredients:

- 2 roma tomatoes
- 2 tomatillos
- 1 (or 2) serrano peppers depending on your spice preference level
- 1 garlic clove, peeled
- 1 tablespoon of salt

Directions:

- Warm a comal at medium heat.
- As the comal heats, rinse all vegetables.
- Once the comal is warm, place the vegetables on it, and keep an eye on them. You want to char them evenly on each side. They will start to dance, which is a good sign. Once they are evenly charred, you can turn off the comal.
- Put the vegetables (minus the chile stem) and salt in a blender. (Make sure your blender can tolerate warm ingredients.)
- Carefully remove the lid of the blender and pour the salsa into a bowl.

  Enjoy this salsa in soups, with chips, or as a garnish—however you love to enjoy salsa!

SUPERFOOD GUACAMOLE

It may seem funny to talk about a restaurant in a cookbook, but to me eating is all about congregating with family around traditional foods. And this particular family memory lingers in my mind and emerges every time I make my own guacamole at home. Growing up, my family and I would go out to eat about once a week. We always went out on my dad's suggestion to change things up a bit, and give my mom a well-deserved break from her beloved kitchen.

There were a few local restaurants on our rotation, but there is one Mexican restaurant in particular that we liked to visit. Fun fact: I still go there as an adult for a date night with el Willy. Or sometimes he and I meet my parents for a drink (when I am able to drink).

My dad, who I lovingly refer to as Monchi, claimed that this restaurant was close by and offered good portions for good prices. Never mind that they had delicious margaritas, ice cold beer, and tableside guacamole. Ah, yes, the ever-famed tableside guacamole. Monchi always makes sure to pay extra for the tableside guacamole: "That way you know it's fresh."

There is something so charming about seeing the green avocados, cilantro and chiles, along with red tomatoes and white onions mixed together in the restaurant's molcajete: the colors of the Mexican flag, dancing together to create an exquisite salsa. The word molcajete itself is rooted in the ancient Nahuatl words mollicaxtli and temolcaxitl, roughly meaning stone mortar for mole or sauce.

Avocados are an excellent source of healthy fats (omega 3s), plus they are chock full of vitamins like vitamins C, E, K and B-6. When avocado toast became a trend, and was hyped for its health benefits, I realized that I've been enjoying nutrients from avocados my whole life in some good, old-fashioned guacamole. Good thing I like guacamole too, because I don't care much for avocado toast, but I sure do love some vitamins and omegas. Therefore, it is my conclusion that guacamole is a superfood.

Guacamole itself works on a lot of levels. You can make it as an appetizer at your next dinner party so that your friends can enjoy it with margaritas before the rest of the food comes out; it can work as a garnish on top of tostadas; or it can work as a side dish. Go ahead, dip some taquitos into your guac! Finally, guacamole also works wonderfully as a snack. I decided to include this guacamole recipe in the salsa section because I tend to eat guacamole the same way I would eat salsa: as a snack, garnish, or an accompaniment to any meal.

If you have a molcajete, you can really throw down old-school style, and serve the guacamole out of the molcajete at your next reunion for a beautiful presentation and for señora cred. If you don't have a molcajete, no worries! Just mash up the avocado with your favorite ingredients.

 FAST
Less than
15 minutes.

 DIFFICULTY
EASY
¡Facilísimo!

 SERVES
6

Ingredients:

- 2 avocados
- 1 or 2 roma tomatoes
- 1 serrano pepper
- 1 handful of cilantro
- 1 small onion
- 2 limes
- Salt, al gusto

Directions:

- Rinse the vegetables.
- Cut the avocado in halves and scoop out the good stuff.
- Place it into a bowl and start mashing it to your desired texture: smooth or chunky.
- Chop the tomato and onion so they are roughly the same size.
- Mince the cilantro.
- Finely chop the chili and make sure you remove the veins and seeds.
- Mix the chopped ingredients into the mashed avocado.
- Add lime and salt, al gusto.

¡BUEN PROVECHO!

BEVERAGES INTRODUCTION

To me, drinking is a vital part of eating. I cannot sit down to enjoy a meal if I don't have the right drink to accompany my dish. I could totally enjoy a drink without a meal, but I could never enjoy a meal without a drink. After all, what is a prime cut of medium-rare steak without a delicious glass of red wine? What is a sunny afternoon without a cold refreshment on the back porch? Drinks bring to mind times spent with friends over guacamole and margaritas, or nachos and cold beers.

When it comes to cooking, I am the expert in my marriage, but my husband is the beverage master. He prefers his drinks to be on the sweeter side, and I prefer mine to be more sour. Together, we love to experiment at home with all sorts of cocktails. (We probably look like mad scientists sometimes!) Our goal is always to find the perfect marriage between sweet and sour.

I hope you enjoy these beverage recipes! Cheers to finding the right balance in your cocktail, marriage, and life. ¡Salud!

HERENCIA COCKTAIL

I must say, many life changes occurred during this book's writing process. For instance, half way through writing it, my marriage was blessed with a pregnancy (our first)! So here I am, reading back through the cocktail recipes that I wrote and tested out before I became pregnant. It's a funny feeling (since I can't drink them now)!

I want you to know that this book was written during small moments that I could find after work, before the gym, or on weekends and holidays. Basically, it took me about a year to write this book. I also didn't write the recipes in the order you see them now; I just wrote things as they came to my mind or as I cooked them for dinner. This particular cocktail recipe I am about to share is one of the last recipes I am adding to the book.

El Willy has made the "very noble sacrifice" of tasting and testing this recipe for me since I am pregnant and, therefore, unable to drink. Who better to help me with this recipe than him? After all, as I said earlier, I claim to be the cooking expert in this marriage; he claims to be the cocktail expert.

Plus, this specific recipe was el Willy's idea. As I was developing this book, he said something like this to me: "Bernie, you have a lot of recipes that are exclusively Salvadorian and exclusively Mexican. You need a recipe that's uniquely all your own; something that embodies what it is to be SalviMex."

And so, this cocktail was created by the both of us. We wanted to combine two ingredients that were particularly unique to each, the Mexican and the Savadorian diet. Tequila is quintessentially Mexican. Nances are unique tropical fruits from El Salvador (and Central America) that can be easily found here in Los Angeles at Latin supermarkets. Why not mix these two together in a drink?

The result is a sweet and sour drink that is reminiscent of a spiked agua fresca or a tropical fruit margarita. I consider it to be the perfect balance of what it means to be SalviMex in Los Angeles.

El Willy and I created this recipe together, but only he has had the opportunity to taste it so far. Con el favor de Dios, by the time the book is published, the baby will be born and I will be able to celebrate the release of this book with an Herencia Cocktail!

I hope you enjoy this drink as much as el Willy does, and as much as I expect to!

MEDIUM
More than 30 minutes.

DIFFICULTY
MODERATE
You got this!

SERVES **4**

Ingredients:

- 1 cup of nances
- 4 shots of tequila, one for each cocktail
- Salt, one pinch
- 2 lemons
- 1 lime
- Sugar (I like 4 teaspoons. My suegra likes 4 tablespoons. So, add gradually and taste often until you reach your desired flavor!)
- Chamoy (enough for the rim of your glass)
- Tajin (enough for the rim of your glass)
- 1 tablespoon of apple cider vinegar
- Ice for your drink
- 4 cups of filtered water to make the fresco (I've added too much water and too little nance base in the past, and the drink comes out too watery. So, I find that 1 cup of nance to 4 cups of water ratio works well!)

Directions:

To make the nance fresco.

This also works as a fresco if you do not drink alcohol

- Rinse the nances well.
- Mix cold water and apple cider vinegar in a bowl and allow the nances to rest in this mixture for about three minutes.
- Drain the nances and rinse well! We don't want a lingering vinegar taste! (Now is a good time to save a couple of cleaned nances to garnish your cocktails.)
- Smoosh the nances in a bowl.
- Add the four cups of filtered water to the smooshed nances. This will be the base of your drink. Allow them to sit for a few moments.
- Run through a colander into a pitcher, using a rubber spatula or your hands to really push the nance pulp through the strainer. The seeds will stay in the strainer.
- Stir the mixture in the pitcher well.

- Squeeze lemon and lime into the pitcher.
- Add a pinch of salt to balance out the sweet and sour flavors.
- Add the sugar, al gusto, to have a yummy sweet and sour mix.
- Stir well (until salt and sugar are dissolved).
- You should have a refreshment that looks like lemonade at this moment.

To make the cocktail.
- Rim your cocktail glass with chamoy and tajin.
- In a cocktail shaker glass, add one shot of tequila, 1 cup of your nance fresco and a handful of ice.
- Shake well.
- Pour into your rimmed glass.
- Plop one nance inside as a garnish.

¡Salud!

SUMMER WATER

Is there anything better than a cold, delicious drink on a summer day? Let's picture the whole image: it's a hot day and you're at a family reunion in someone's backyard. There are vibrant tablecloths covering the outdoor tables, and the children are chasing each other, laughing, and shouting. Some comadres are gossiping and fanning themselves. The señora, who is not technically your tía but whom you call tía anyway, just brought out a tray of fruta picada. Someone is grilling the carne asada. You're absolutely thirsty in the heat, so you guzzle down something ice cold and satisfying, maybe it's an agua fresca with extra ice that your "tía" lovingly made. Now, you feel refreshed.

As I write this, I recall my childhood: hot summer days spent outdoors at carne asadas with my immediate and extended family and family friends. I grew up in South East LA where it is basically always summer. In the heat, I like to drink something refreshing and crisp. Now that I am an adult, I want to make sure that my summer beverages are offering me extra hydration, without compromising flavor.

I also like drinks that are low in calories; I do not like to drink my calories. If you want a sugar-free agua recipe, then this is a great option for you! This drink was inspired by the early days of my career working in the spa industry, in my 20s. After tasting so many different types over the years, I developed my personal favorite type of spa water. Crisp, clean, and tangy. Refreshing. Satisfying. Enjoy it on a warm day or make it and bring it to the next carne asada you attend. Presume or show off to all your tías that you made your own agua fresca that is low in calories and tastes good, para cuidarte la forma, pues. If you're hanging out with your adult friends, spike it with your favorite tequila blanco. Drink the non-alcoholic version the next day when you're hungover. ('Cause hey, balance, OK?) There are so many ways to enjoy this drink!

FAST
Less than
15 minutes.

DIFFICULTY
EASY
¡Facilísimo!

SERVES
10

Ingredients:

- Filtered water
- 1 cucumber
- 1 or 2 lemons
- A handful of mint leaves

Directions:

- Wash and dry all the produce.
- Peel the cucumber.
- Cut the cucumber into medium-sized slices and put them into your pitcher.
- Add mint leaves.
- Add lemon juice, avoid adding any seeds.
- Pour water over the ingredients, into the pitcher.
- Stir.
- Refrigerate for an hour so that the flavors can steep into the water.
- Serve over ice and enjoy!

TEQUILA ON THE ROCKS

When I visited Mexico City in 2019, I made a point to visit the pyramids of Teotihuacan. There, I learned that my ancestors created pulque (which is basically like warrior Moon Shine) out of maguey, which is a type of agave plant. The Teotihuacanos were so amazed by the effects of pulque, that they came to the consensus that gods must exist. After all, who but the gods themselves could create something as magical as the feeling that pulque (or really any booze) provides? Yes, believe it or not, the feeling of being buzzed is what led our ancestors to believe in divine beings!

Considering that we Latinxs are descendants of nations such as the Teotihuacan Empire, it comes as no surprise that my tíos, parents, cousins, husband, cuñados and I all love to turn up with a certain drink that is also derived from agave— tequila. Think about it. Even the toughest or most stoic relative gets gushy after a few shots of tequila while listening to some good songs. Tequila enjoyed in good company, in my experience, has led to happy drunks hugging each other over and over again, singing along to music, or reminiscing about old memories while making new ones.

My personal drink of choice is almost always tequila, regardless of the occasion. I feel shy admitting this in a book where I am putting together sophisticated recipes/beverages, but when I first started drinking, I would drink tequila with Squirt soda (keeping it real here). I must admit that, to this day, if one of my favorite cousins hands me tequila with Squirt and chamoy at a family reunion, I will probably (that is, definitely) accept. All the same, my metabolism has slowed down over the years, so to avoid soda yet still taste something that will make me pucker, I began drinking tequila with lime juice on the rocks.

It has taken some trial and error, but I have perfected the recipe. It is absolutely delicious, satisfying, and relatively low in carbs and calories! I am trying to save my carbs for the late-night tacos, if you know what I mean.

FAST
Less than 10 minutes.

DIFFICULTY
EASY
¡Facilísimo!

SERVES
1

Ingredients:

- 1 oz high quality sipping tequila, like Clase Azul
- 1 oz lime juice
- Chamoy, to taste
- Tajin, to taste
- Ice, enough to fill your glass

Directions:

- Prepare the rim of your favorite drinking glass with chamoy and Tajin.
- Put ice into the glass.
- Pour in 1 oz (one shot) of your favorite sipping tequila.
- Pour in 1 oz of lime juice.

Señora Advice

*I used to love to sprinkle salt on lemons and suck on them as a child. This drink is salty and sour and reminds me of that! If you like sour things, you will love it. If you are not a fan of things that are too sour, you can always add a splash of agave to balance out the strong lime flavor.

TEQUILA TODDY

Hilarious Mexican comedian Sophia Nino de Rivera tells a joke where she admits she is becoming a señora. For instance, she asks for her Tupperware containers back and is shocked when others go out without a sweater. Do you know what I'm talking about here? Do you find yourself telling others to put on shoes to avoid being barefoot inside the house, or advise against going out with wet hair? As I enter my thirties, I can definitely relate. There are a lot of examples in my own life, but one in particular stands out: I now have my own special remedy to soothe a sore throat.

Allow me to tell you how this came to be. At first, to soothe a sore throat, I would down a shot of tequila con un chingo de lime juice. After that, to replace tequila and avoid getting drunk, I'd sip on hot water with lemon and honey. I had heard of Hot Toddy, which is like a hot whiskey tea-like beverage that is great for colds, but I am not really a whiskey gal. I am, and always will be, a tequila type of woman.

So, I thought about it a bit and realized that if I drink Mexican Mules instead of Moscow Mules all the time, why not make a Mexican Hot Toddy? A Tequila Toddy if you will. After some trial and error, I put together something that my loved ones and I enjoy quite a bit! Now, it's my go-to sore throat remedy, and it works as a tasty drink on cold days.

There are a few things to keep in mind with this recipe: you want to be able to sip on this beverage, so tequilas like Don Julio Silver or Patron Silver will make it smoother. And the key is to really mix the ingredients together before you pour in the hot water. Once you pour in the hot water, continue to stir. You will find that everything melts together.

So, whether you want to get your buzz on with a warm drink in the cold months or you want something to soothe your throat, this is the drink for you.

FAIRLY FAST
About 15 minutes.

DIFFICULTY
EASY to MEDIUM

SERVES 1

Ingredients:

- 1 shot of tequila
- 2 tablespoons of organic or raw honey
- The juice of a whole, large lemon
- 1 cinnamon stick
- 2 cloves
- 2 cups of water
- A pinch of cayenne pepper, optional

Directions:

- Put water to boil.
- Pour the lemon juice and honey into your mug. Mix well.
- Add the tequila into the mug and stir.
- If using cayenne, add it at this point.
- Continue to stir until you are satisfied that the three ingredients are well mixed. Add the two cloves to the mixture.
- Put the cinnamon stick into the mug in a standing position.
- Once boiled, pour the hot water into the mug.
- Stir everything with the cinnamon stick to bring out all the flavors.

¡Salud!

SMOKEY PALOMITA

FAST
Less than 10 minutes.

DIFFICULTY
EASY
¡Facilísimo!

SERVES
1

I know I am not the first person to suggest drinking mezcal with grapefruit juice, but oh boy! I did feel like a genius when I tasted the two flavors together for the first time! El Willy and I had gone out with close friends the night before and had a little too much fun.

The next day, we skipped the gym and slept in. Feeling hungover, we had a huge brunch: lots of potatoes and toast to soak up the tequila from the previous evening. I knew I needed some of "the hair of the dog that bit me" to recover, but I wasn't quite in the mood for a michelada, and I'm not really a mimosa type of girl. However, I love grapefruit juice and I love mezcal, so I decided to try those two together. Mezcal, to keep the buzz going (remember I said this book is only semi healthy! Don't judge me) and grapefruit juice for vitamins and refreshment. I poured it over ice and threw in a mint leaf to feel fancy. Wow! The bittersweet citrus of the juice! The smokiness of the mezcal! The ice to make it extra crisp and refreshing! Even the tiny mint leaf played its part. My newest favorite drink was born.

This drink is great at brunch or on a summer day. When it comes to alcohol, remember that balance and moderation is best, and according to many studies one drink a day can help your heart. Cheers to that!

Show off this cocktail next time you host brunch for your homies. It can be your Latin take on a mimosa, or a new twist on a traditional paloma.

Ingredients:

- 1 shot of mezcal
- 1 cup of grapefruit juice, fresh
- A few mint leaves, to garnish
- Ice, as much as you would like

Directions:

- Pour ice into a glass.
- Pour the mezcal and juice into the glass.
- Stir.
- Garnish with a mint leaf.

¡Salud!

AGUA DE HIBISCUS

MEDIUM
More than
30 minutes.
You'll need
to wait for the
concentrate to cool.

DIFFICULTY
MEDIUM
Get ready to
have fun in the
kitchen!

SERVES
10

Hibiscus has a lot of benefits. It can keep blood pressure low, it is diuretic (I feel like I lose water weight any time I drink straight hibiscus tea), and it's also great for bladder and kidney health. I find myself drinking hibiscus tea instead of cranberry juice when I'm concerned with my bladder health. (But, FYI, pregnant women should avoid hibiscus.)

I mentioned earlier in this section that I don't particularly like to drink my calories: I drink my coffee black, my tea unsweetened, and I also tend to add very little mixers to my liquor. For these reasons, I don't often drink aguas frescas because they're at times so sugary. However, it's hard to turn down my suegra's agua de Jamaica. It's too tasty. She makes it just right!

When it comes to sugary drinks like these, I enjoy them thoughtfully and in moderation. My logic is, everyone wants a sweet drink now and then. Why buy sodas for my Sunday carne asada with the fam when I can make them a homemade drink and know exactly what's in it?

My suegra taught me her recipe a while back. Now, I make it at home for myself with less sugar, and it comes out a bit more tart (but I personally love tart things). When I serve it, I make sure to include a lot of ice and garnish it with a squeeze of lime. I playfully call my take on it, agua de hibiscus. Now, add some vodka and you're good! Just kidding! This is great on its own. (However, who am I to judge if you decide to add vodka to this?)

Ingredients:

- Water, to dilute the hibiscus concentrate
- 2 cups of hibiscus flowers
- Sugar, al gusto
- Lime juice

Directions:

- Rinse the flowers in a colander.
- After washing them, place the flowers in a bowl of cool water. Allow them to rest for a moment.
- Take flowers out of the bowl with your hand and put them in a pot of water on the stove. As you move the flowers from the bowl to the pot, you may see some deposits in the bowl of water. This is why it is so necessary to rinse.
- Bring water to boil at medium heat.
- Once it boils, turn the flame off and cover the pot.
- Let the flowers seep in the water as the water cools down. This creates the hibiscus concentrate.
- Once the hibiscus concentrate cools down, run through a colander into your pitcher.
- Take the time to squeeze extra moisture out of flowers.
- Add sugar to taste and more water as needed.

Enjoy over ice with a garnish of lime!

Señora Advice

*You can freeze the concentrate and save it to make some of this beverage later.

SALVI ENSALADA

FAIRLY FAST
About 15 Minutes.

DIFFICULTY
EASY
Chop, mix, pour, and you are set!

SERVES
10

For those of you who are not Salvadorian, you may be thinking, did Bernie make a mistake? Why is there a salad in the beverage section? For those of you who are Salvadorian, you already know what I am talking about!

This recipe is actually a popular Salvadorian beverage. It is a drinkable fruit salad. It is a sweet fruit punch with finely chopped fruit, such as apple or mango, floating in it. It is known by many names such as refresco de ensalada de frutas, fresco de ensalada, or agua de ensalada. Most of the time, it is simply called ensalada to keep it short and sweet.

Speaking of sweetness, this is indeed a sweet drink. Sometimes, if I buy it from the store, I have to water it down to balance out the sweetness.

I remember my mother used to make fresh ensalada and serve it in an elegant-looking punch bowl. The way she made it, it was never too sweet. It was just right. She would lovingly serve me the drink in a cup, and I would find such joy in munching on the little pieces of floating fruit. The diced apples mamá used were always perfect and offered the most satisfying crisp as I bit into them.

Out of all my siblings, I would get the most excited when she made this, on what seemed to be rare occasions. In fact, she says that, out of all her kids, I love her Salvadorian recipes the most. No wonder I married a Salvadorian-American! (All of my siblings married Mexican-Americans.)

As you can see, the recipe I included here contains apples, oranges, pineapple, and mango. I like to use what is in season and what is available. However, I encourage you to use your favorite fruit!

Ingredients:

- 2 cans of pineapple
- 2 granny smith apples
- 1 mango (Make sure it is not too ripe or mushy. Crunchier mangos work great here.)
- 2 oranges, the juicer, the better!
- 1 lemon
- Water

Directions:

- Wash the apples, oranges and mango.
- Finely dice the apple and place it in your pitcher. (You can use a food processor here. I certainly do!)
- Squeeze lemon over the diced apples to prevent them from turning brown. (Use a strainer to avoid adding any lemon seeds.)
- Finely dice the mango and add to your pitcher.
- Open both cans of pineapples and drain out the syrup. (I do not like using the syrup from the can. It is way too sweet in my opinion.)
- Finely dice the fruit from one can.
- Place the fruit from the second can in a blender to get a beautiful pineapple juice.
- Add the juiced pineapple and diced pineapple to your pitcher.
- Squeeze the juice from your oranges into your pitcher. (Again, a strainer works great here.)
- Fill the rest of your punch bowl with filtered water and stir.
- Refrigerate for at least an hour before enjoying so that the flavors can really blend together.

Stir and enjoy!

Señora Advice

*Enjoy this drink on its own on a hot day, or as an accompaniment to your favorite Salvadorian dish. I love this drink with pupusas!

*You will see I made this recipe without added sugar. The fruit is sweet enough in my opinion! Taste it and see for yourself.

BREAKFAST INTRODUCTION

I want this book to add value to our lives in many ways. And something that is important to me is choosing nutritious and convenient options for my meals. I wish this breakfast section included huevos con weenies or chilaquiles, but the fact of the matter is that those should probably not be eaten every morning for breakfast. When I do enjoy that sort of thing, it is typically on a special occasion or on a weekend, and I savor every bite.

Aside from that, do you have any idea of how early I would have to wake up to make something like chilaquiles every morning? I am a working woman on the go. Some mornings I wake up, work out, shower, and get ready for work (i.e., I do my hair and makeup). On those mornings, I need to grab something fast, convenient, and satisfying.

This is where this particular section comes into play. After all, breakfast is the most important meal of the day, and I try my best to be intentional with what I put in my body first thing in the morning, en ayunas, even if I am short of time. Read on for recipes that will start you off on the right track, fit into an on-the-go lifestyle, and taste delicious!

BERNIE'S SIGNATURE BLUEBERRY SMOOTHIE

FAST
About 10 minutes.
It's quick enough
to make on busy
mornings!

DIFFICULTY
EASY
¡Facilísimo!

SERVES 1

Smoothies are my favorite go-to weekday breakfast. I genuinely find joy in making myself a smoothie every morning. The reason why I like to make them myself instead of buying them is because I know exactly what is in it: real fruit, not fruit juice.

After blending my smoothie, I throw it in a mason jar with a lid and a silicon or stainless-steel straw. Then I am good to go! I love the convenience of sipping my smoothie on my commute to work or even at my desk while working. So many coworkers have asked me where I bought my smoothie, only to be amazed that I made it myself. But, as beautiful and vibrant as my smoothies look, they really do not require much effort!

I always use frozen fruit for my smoothies. This way, they won't go bad as quickly, plus it saves me time as I don't have to spend extra time chopping fruit or adding ice. When choosing frozen fruit, I prefer berries because they are lower in sugar and higher in fiber.

I also use 0% fat Greek yogurt, which is way more affordable and easier to digest than protein powders. Plus, it has natural probiotics. For omegas and fiber, I add chia seeds. Chia proves that big things come in small packages. They are considered a superfood nowadays, and they were the superfood of our Aztec ancestors. Wow! I made a healthy breakfast and honored my ancestors all before 9 a.m. That is the type of vibe I am all about.

Sometimes, I throw in a splash of coconut water for electrolytes.

Superfoods ready to nourish your body first thing in the morning plus the added convenience and flavor, what is not to love?

Ingredients:
- 1 tablespoon of chia seeds
- 1 cup of frozen blueberries
- 1 cup of 0% fat, unflavored and unsweetened Greek yogurt
- 1 cup of water
- 1 splash of coconut water, optional

Directions:
- Add all the ingredients to a blender.
- Blend until you reach your desired consistency.

Pour smoothie into a reusable cup with a lid and straw, and enjoy!

GREEN SMOOTHIE

You know, I love smoothies so much that I included two of them in this section. This one will come in handy if you are trying to get in more greens. It contains pineapple for enzymes and sweetness. It also includes spinach or kale for vitamins, fiber, and folic acid. I also throw in some chia seeds for omegas, protein, and healthy fat (and 'cause it reminds me that I am an Aztec warrior!). Finally, it includes 0% fat Greek yogurt for protein and probiotics.

The pineapple really hides the taste of the spinach if you are still transitioning into eating more greens, or don't particularly love the taste of greens. Drink this smoothie in the morning and get ahead of your fruit, vegetables, omegas, and protein servings. What is not to love?

My husband taught me this recipe. When we first moved in together, we invested in a fancy blender so that we could make healthy smoothies for breakfast every morning. This green smoothie is the first smoothie I made when my husband and I were starting our lives together and joining our daily routines. The first few months of living together were so fun. Mostly because we quickly realized we didn't have to drive back and forth to hang out with each other—we were already hanging out in our own casa! So, somehow, it happened that the fancy blender was initially used for margaritas every night. (Hey, we didn't have to drive anywhere!) There we were—drinking margaritas by night and having healthy smoothies in the morning. Such personifications of health...

I almost called this the hangover smoothie because of this memory. But, to keep the recipe as family-friendly as possible, and so that y'all won't think I am a borracha, let's call it the green smoothie. It's lean and green, and will keep you full until lunch!

FAST
About 10 minutes. It's quick enough to make on busy mornings!

DIFFICULTY
EASY
¡Facilísimo!

SERVES
1

Ingredients:

- 1 cup of spinach or kale. (Spinach is milder and kale is earthier, so keep that in mind.)
- 1 cup of frozen pineapple
- 1 cup of Greek yogurt
- 1 tablespoon of chia seeds
- 1 cup of water
- 1 splash of coconut water, optional

Directions:

- Add all the ingredients into a blender.
- Blend until smooth or until you reach your desired consistency.

Pour smoothie into a reusable cup with a lid and straw, and enjoy!

OVERNIGHT OATS

FAST
About 10 minutes of prep time.

DIFFICULTY
EASY
This is bachelor-level easy.

SERVES 1

I have a theory that bachelors have the best cooking hacks. No frills. All efficiency. They are meal prepping masters. I recall visiting my brother when he was a bachelor. He lived off of boiled chicken breast and potatoes. Flavor? Who needs flavor when you have easy cooking? Needless to say, my mom left some salt and spices at his place after one visit in hopes that he would adopt some seasoning techniques soon.

OK, so yes, some efficient cooking may lack flavor, but not always. After all, my bro has since become a grilling master who would not be caught compromising flavor.

This recipe, in particular, is inspired by el WIlly's best friend (who happens to be SalviMex too, like me!). I love the homie dearly (and regularly punk him) like he was my own brother. When el Willy and I were remodeling our house, we stayed with him, in a detached rental unit on the same lot of his house. We often cooked together and shared cooking hacks with each other.

The homie wakes up at 5 a.m. to go to work, so he doesn't necessarily want to wake up even earlier to prepare a meal. Understandable. His go-to breakfast? Overnight oats

If you use the right amount of ingredients, you can ensure that all the food groups are included in your meal: protein, healthy fats, carbs, and fruits. The key is to use frozen fruit: that way, you can leave the oats on the counter and grab them to go in the morning, and your fruit will still be fresh. After all, there are enough things to remember on busy mornings. And I cannot tell you how many times I've forgotten my lunch or breakfast in the fridge!

Ingredients:

- 1/2 cup of oatmeal
- 1/2 cup of frozen fruit of your choice
- 1 handful of granola or nuts of your choice
- 1 pinch of chia seeds
- 1 cup of almond milk, enough to cover the dry ingredients

Directions:

- In the evening, put the oats into your container.
- Top with fruit.
- Add in the granola or nuts and seeds.
- Add the milk.
- Close the lid tightly and shake.
- Keep the lid tightly closed and leave the container on the counter, or in the fridge.

Enjoy the following morning!

Señora Advice

*You can use the Nut Clusters from the snack section in this book in place of granola.

PROTEIN PARFAIT

If you had told me ten years ago that, one day, I would be writing a Latinx cookbook with some semi-healthy recipes, I would have told you that you were trippin'. Yes, I have always loved writing. Yes, my culture has always been a very important part of my identity. But eating healthy? No way. I am the girl who survived off chips and energy drinks for longer than I would like to admit. However, my metabolism began to slow down toward my mid-twenties and I could no longer hang. Esas comidas empezaron a caerme pasadas. My body could not break them down like it used to, and I felt tired all the time. This was around the time my husband and I started dating. As a lifelong athlete, he was very influential in my "health journey."

I remember I would ask him every question you could think of. As I share this recipe, one memory, in particular, comes to mind: "What's the deal with Greek yogurt?" I asked, "Why is it so hyped up?" He responded by telling me that it was due to the higher protein content. So, there I was, twenty-three and buying Greek yogurt, sweetened, with all the artificial color and flavor that probably trumped the yogurt's benefits of calcium, probiotics, and protein.

Well, trial and error is just human, right? So, if something like this has happened to you, do not get discouraged. Take it as a learning lesson, move on, and make the necessary little tweaks. Small changes that we stick with long-term will offer more results than huge sweeping changes that are not sustainable over time.

It took me a while to come to the realization, but once I did, I switched to 0% unsweetened Greek yogurt. I have used it exclusively ever since. I use it in my smoothies, and I use it in this particular recipe too.

Alright, so with that said, let's get to this recipe! I eat it for breakfast, but sometimes, I will have it for dinner on a Sunday evening when I want something light after an indulgent weekend.

I like this recipe because it is so customizable. For instance, the fruit I suggested can be swapped out for your personal favorites. You can also use your favorite nuts instead of the suggested ones.

FAST
About 10 minutes.

DIFFICULTY
EASY
¡Facilísimo!

SERVES 1

Ingredients:

- 1 cup of unsweetened Greek yogurt
- 1 cup of chopped fruit of your choice. I recommend berries or something in season
- 1 tablespoon of chopped nuts, like slivered almonds
- 1 pinch of chia seeds
- 1 teaspoon of vanilla extract
- 1 tablespoon of organic honey, optional

Directions:

- Wash and, if applicable, cut the fruit.
- Put the Greek yogurt into a bowl.
- Stir the vanilla extract into the yogurt to add some flavor.
- Top with the fruit, nuts and seeds.
- Taste it and add honey if you desire more sweetness.

¡Buen provecho!

MONCHI'S OMELET

MODERATE
Less than 30 minutes.
You can enjoy this on
a slow-paced Sunday
morning.

DIFFICULTY
**MEDIUM TO
DIFFICULT**
if you ask me.
Easy to medium,
if you ask Monchi.

SERVES
1

Yogurt and oats are a great breakfast on the go, sure. Sometimes, however, I want a hot meal for breakfast, especially on the weekends or on a cold morning to warm up my body before leaving home.

I cannot share this recipe without recalling one of my favorite recent memories. OK, so this may sound crazy coming from the author of a cookbook, but making omelets intimidates the heck out of me. Most of my omelets basically end up coming out as scrambles.

My father (aka Monchi), on the other hand, is an omelet flipping master. (What can I say? My dad learned a thing or two from my Nana.) One Father's Day weekend, my husband and I visited my parents on Saturday for a carne asada. We hung out, drank, and then my husband and I spent the night. On Sunday morning, after waking up, the four of us (my parents, spouse, and I) had breakfast before Sunday mass.

There I was whipping up some eggs to ensure they would be extra fluffy. At that moment, Monchi came in and I told him, "Hey, since you're so much better at flipping omelets than I am, you wanna take a whack at this?" ¡No me digas! The poor guy ended up making everyone else's omelets—on Father's Day!

According to Monchi, I manipulated him that morning. According to me, I was just giving el don the room to expertly handle business.

I'll let you be the judge.

This scramble is a great way to add some veggies into your body first thing in the morning. Again, these are guidelines. I included vegetables that I personally enjoy. You can customize this recipe by swapping for your favorite veggies. And remember to buy free-range eggs, if you can.

Ingredients:

- 2 egg whites
- 1 whole egg
- 1 handful of spinach, chopped
- 1/4 bell pepper, chopped
- 1/4 onion, chopped
- 1 tablespoon of olive oil for your pan
- A splash of milk for the eggs
- Salt and pepper, al gusto
- Tapatío, for the omelette once its cooked
- 1 pinch of crushed chiltepines for a kick, optional

Directions:

- Wash, rinse and chop the produce.
- In a bowl, whip up the eggs and egg whites. The more you whisk, the fluffier they will be.
- Add in the splash of milk to the eggs and really whip them up. Put your wrist into it!
- Set a pan to warm on the stove. Once warm, apply the oil.
- Lower the flame and pour the egg mix onto the pan.
- With a rubber spatula, lightly lift the edges of the omelet to avoid sticking
- Keep an eye on the egg mixture. You will see it change in color and texture as it cooks.
- Sprinkle chopped veggies on top of egg mix. If using chiltepines, you can add them at this moment too.
- Fold in half.
- Put the flame up to medium/low and cook the folded omelette for about a minute more on each side.
- Shimmy the omelette out of the pan and onto your plate.

Enjoy with some Tapatío!

SNACKS INTRODUCTION

Let's be really honest here: snacking is a simple yet almost perfect pleasure. What is a trip to the movie theater without a bucket of popcorn? How happy did you feel as an adolescent when your mama knocked on your bedroom door to surprise you with fresh-cut fruit? How satisfying is it to grab a few nuts when you arrive home after training at the gym and feel extremely hungry? Finally, happy hour margaritas are not the same without the ever-famed bottomless chips and salsa. Who doesn't love snacking?

I recall when I lived with my parents, and my husband and I were still dating. El Willy would come over with any offering he thought I would enjoy—my favorite chips, my favorite candy, or some tacos from King Taco. We would rent a movie and chill on the couch and nibble away. Even now that we are married, we look forward to streaming a movie or catching up on a show on a Sunday afternoon with yummy snacks.

Snacking is fun! Yet, depending on what you are snacking on, it may or may not be the best habit. I could eat all the candy I wanted when I was twenty-three and first dating my husband. Now that I am thirty, I try to be careful with what I eat. I want to live a long comfortable life so that I can be around for my children, and, someday, my grandchildren! I want to feel strong so I can be there for my parents and my husband. Most of all, I want to feel my best so I can be there for myself!

So how do I continue to enjoy the pleasure of snacking while still ensuring I make the best choices for myself? I eat snacks that are good for me and that taste delicious, of course! The snacks I included in this section are some of my very favorites. They are fun to make, full of nutrients, and full of flavor. I hope they bring you as much joy as they bring me.

CUCUMBER PICADO

FAST
Less than
10 minutes.

DIFFICULTY
EASY
¡Facilísimo!

SERVES
1

Salt and lemon are the sun and moon of my palate. As a matter of fact, as a child, I used to suck on lemons that had a tiny sprinkle of salt on them. RIP, tooth enamel. When I enjoy lemon and salt today, I tell myself that lemons are full of vitamin C and that salt is an electrolyte.

I love salt and lemon so much that, for a long time, the only way I would eat vegetables would be if they were crunchy and dressed with lemon and salt. Cucumbers. Jicama. Salads. You get the idea.

If you are like me, you already know what's up with this type of snack—maybe you mix some fruit and veggies in a bowl with lime juice, Tajín, and a touch of chamoy. If you don't, then get ready to enjoy the world's tastiest and simplest snack.

Remember this easy recipe when you're struggling to get more veggies in your diet. Vegetables do not have to be boring. When you catch yourself getting sick of steamed broccoli, come back to some raw veggies with Tajín and lemon.

This is a simple recipe because that's what this book is about. We are eating foods that remind us of our culture, which we love so much, all while "heathifying" our lifestyles just a bit. My goal is to do all this without over-complicating things. I hope you enjoy this simple recipe, and perhaps even remember other familiar snacks that are also delicious and nutritious options.

Ingredients:

- 1 large cucumber
- 1 large lemon
- A pinch of tajin

Directions:

- Rinse the cucumber.
- Cut off the tip and rub it against the rest of the cucumber, you will see emulsification. This removes any bitterness from the cucumber.
- When you finish, rinse the cucumber again and throw the tip away.
- Peel the cucumber.
- Slice the cucumber to your taste. Thicker slices are more crunchy; thinner slices soak up more lime juice.
- Put the sliced cucumber into a bowl.
- Squeeze lemon all over and mix.
- Sprinkle on some Tajín.

¡Buen provecho!

SPICY POPCORN

Popcorn is crunchy, salty, and fun to eat. Additionally, five cups of popcorn contain the same amount of carbs as one cup of corn chips. Popcorn will offer a little more fiber as well. I personally like to make it at home, so that I can control the ingredients. I like to know exactly what is going into my body, so I can make conscious choices. Plus, when I make it at home, I can control the flavor. Tajín, anyone?

Popping your own popcorn is a great party trick. Invite bae over for a movie night and pop some popcorn to show them you are wifey (or hubby) material, invite your nephews over and totally blow their minds when you pop corn on the stovetop, or simply pop it for yourself when you want a snack that you can enjoy.

Whomever you make it for, remember your ancestors when you eat it: maíz was a huge part of our warrior ancestor's diet. Remember who you are when you eat corn, just keep in mind that there is so much controversy about corn and GMO! So, make sure you get yourself some non-GMO kernels, and then enjoy every bite.

I'd also like to add that I experimented with a lot of different types of oils to pop my popcorn. I find that coconut oil works best. And, instead of salt, I season it with Tajín. Everybody who knows me knows that I can basically put Tajín on anything.

Squeezing lemon juice over the popcorn is completely optional, but, if you chose to do it, remember that less is more. No one wants soggy popcorn!

FAST
Less than 10 minutes. This is super quick!

DIFFICULTY
EASY TO MEDIUM

SERVES 2

Ingredients:

- 2 tablespoons of refined coconut oil
- 1/2 cup of popcorn kernels
- Tajín, al gusto, for seasoning

Directions:

- In a medium, heavy-bottomed saucepan, over medium heat, add oil and two popcorn kernels. Cover the pot.
- When these two kernels pop, the oil is at the best temperature to make your popcorn.
- While you wait, get a large bowl ready.
- Once the two test kernels pop, turn off the burner. Remove pot from the heat and add the rest of the kernels.
- Put the pot back on the burner, occasionally shimmying the pot.
- Once the kernels start popping, tip the lid to allow steam to escape.
- Wait for the popping to slow down and turn off the burner.
- Remove the lid and pour the popcorn into a serving bowl.
- Season with Tajín.

¡Buen provecho!

ORTEGA MOLINA NUT CLUSTERS

One night, el Willy came home with a bottle of wine and a prepackaged little snack from the wine shop. The snack consisted of different nuts rolled in brown rice syrup (and other sweeteners) and seasoned with ginger. It paired with the wine wonderfully. Then, it made my (super sensitive) stomach hurt. I know my body pretty well, and I was certain the sweeteners hurt my tummy. Bummer because those snacks were so delicious!

Without thinking much about it, I decided to make my own nut clusters the next day. I got some of my favorite nuts: sliced almonds for texture, cashews for crunch, pepitas for color. If the snack is not fun, then I don't want it! I mixed the three different nuts in maple syrup (because I was worried honey would be too sticky), and sprinkled powdered cayenne, cinnamon, and ginger for extra flavor. I put them on a baking sheet with parchment paper, baked them for a few minutes, and hoped for the best.

After they finished baking, I set them out to cool. Then I made dinner. When el Willy came home he asked, "What is that smell? It smells so good!" He tasted the snack, and his pupils might as well have dilated. "You gotta sell these," he said. What a compliment!

Let me tell you, I was so relieved that the first recipe I made on my own from simple inspiration turned out well! It passed el Willy's taste test, that is, it pleased the pickiest of palates. Right then and there, I could feel myself becoming a more experienced home cook. It was definitely a turning point for my confidence in the kitchen.

Now, I make these often when I am entertaining. They are a crowd favorite, and are nutrient dense. Make these for your S.O. (significant other) or your friends next time you're hosting, or take them as an alternative dessert to your next get together. Whichever occasion you make them for, I hope you enjoy them!

MODERATE
About 20-30 minutes.

DIFFICULTY
EASY TO MEDIUM

SERVES 2

Ingredients:
- 1 cup of raw, unroasted mixed nuts: sliced almonds, cashews, and pumpkin seeds
- 3 tablespoons of organic, raw maple syrup
- 1 teaspoon of ground ginger
- 1 teaspoon of cinnamon
- A pinch of cayenne pepper

Directions:
- Preheat the oven to 350 degrees.
- Line a baking sheet with parchment paper.
- In a large bowl, mix the nuts, seeds, maple syrup, and seasonings so that everything is evenly coated.
- Place the nut and seed mixture onto the baking sheet and spread into an even layer.
- Bake for 10-12 minutes.
- Remove from oven.
- Allow to cool for about 15 minutes.
- Once cooled, break apart into bite-size pieces.

¡Buen provecho!

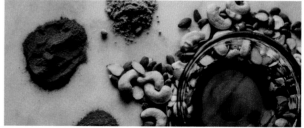

LAZY NACHOS

My twelve-year-old nephew inspired this recipe. He shared with me that he likes nachos but nacho cheese kind of grosses him out. He asked me, "is it even real cheese?" The little homie brought up a good point. I love loaded nachos, and figured I should take a crack at some yummy homemade nachos.

Some things I learned:

I personally prefer blue corn chips because they're different and fun. As for the cheese, you can buy a bag of pre-shredded Mexican cheese blend, or grate your own cheese blocks at home, whatever you have time for. The tastiest cheeses, in my opinion, are cheddar or Monterey Jack. The chips and cheese are the stars of this show, so choose them wisely.

Next, consider the other toppings. You can use leftover or canned beans to make this recipe fairly quickly. (Be sure to always rinse your canned beans first.) You can also use fresh or canned jalapeño peppers. The beans, peppers, and cheese can all go on top of the chips, on the baking tray, straight into the oven. You want all of these to be warm.

After you take the nachos out of the oven, sprinkle on some queso fresco and pico de gallo. My intuition tells me that pico de gallo would be less tasty if baked.

The key is to keep this recipe customizable. For instance, when I make it for my nephew, he's happy with just warm chips and melted cheese. Meanwhile, I want the works on mine. There is no wrong way to enjoy nachos. (Unless you put black olives on them.)

This recipe is a great way to repurpose some leftover beans or salsa into a tasty snack.

FAST
About
15 minutes.

DIFFICULTY
EASY TO
MEDIUM

SERVES
6

Ingredients:
- 1 bag of corn chips
- 2 cups of shredded cheese
- 1 cup of beans, whole and drained
- 1 cup of salsa
- 2 tablespoons of shredded queso fresco
- Sliced chiles, al gusto

Directions:
- Preheat the oven to 350 degrees.
- Line a baking sheet with parchment paper.
- Spread the chips across the baking sheet in an even layer.
- Sprinkle shredded cheese over the chips, coating the chips evenly with cheese.
- Carefully put the beans over the chips and cheese, distributing evenly.
- Top with peppers, if you wish.
- Bake for 5 to 10 minutes, until the cheese is melted but not burnt. Keep an eye on the chips and really watch the cheese.
- Remove the tray from the oven carefully and top with salsa and queso fresco.

KALE CHIPS

I'm writing this book in my free time after work. A lot has happened since I started: my husband and I sold our condo, rented an apartment next door to his best friend, then bought, remodeled, and moved into our current house. Plus, a lot more. As I write today's recipe, I am currently five and a half months pregnant (closer to six, really). And I am craving salty, crispy things.

My husband, el Willy, and I took a nutrition class together to learn about which foods will best nourish our gestating baby boy. A list of superfoods was shared with us, one being kale. No lie, the day after the class, el Willy bought all the foods off the suggested list. Particularly, he came home with more kale than I knew what to do with. (Really, how much salad can one woman eat? Even if she's eating for two.)

I decided to experiment with kale chips. I rinsed the kale, broke it into little pieces, and let them drip dry in a colador. (As I waited, I really wished I had a salad spinner. I bought one a week later.) Then, I patted off any excessive moisture. In a bowl, I mixed the kale with olive oil. I really rubbed the kale, because I've heard massaging the kale with olive oil can diminish any unwanted bitterness. Then I sprinkled some Tajín (like, yo, Tajín just sponsor me already) and gave it all another toss.

A few moments after roasting in the oven, I had a perfectly crispy, salty, and nutritious snack! I ate the whole batch in about ten minutes.

Don't knock it 'till you try it. This is a great way to get more greens in your diet and it tastes so good!

MEDIUM
About 30 minutes.

DIFFICULTY
EASY TO MEDIUM
You'll need to watch the kale in the oven.

SERVES 1

Ingredients:
- Kale, enough so that it evenly covers your baking sheet
- 1 tablespoon of olive oil
- Tajín, al gusto

Directions:
- Preheat the oven to 350 degrees.
- Rinse the kale and remove the leaves from the stems in small bite-size pieces.
- Thoroughly dry the kale. (It must be dry in order to crisp properly.)
- In a bowl, toss the kale with olive oil and Tajín.
- Spread the kale evenly across the baking sheet.
- Bake in the oven for 10 to 15 minutes. Carefully watch the kale those last five minutes to ensure the edges brown but do not burn.
- Remove from the oven, allow it to cool and enjoy!

¡Buen provecho!

MIX & MATCH
LUNCH OR DINNER

This next section of the book is a little different. Before we get to that, though, I want to review the basic components of a balanced meal.

To put it very simply, a balanced meal consists of:

Protein: This macronutrient is essential for building and repairing muscle mass and it's usually found in animal products such as beef, fish, seafood, chicken, pork, eggs, cheese, and many others. Nuts, seeds, and legumes are also a great protein source.

Starches / carbohydrates: Starches and carbohydrates, in general, are what your body needs to make glucose, which is your main source of energy. You can find carbs in grains such as rice, cereal, pan, beans, potato, corn, tortillas, etc.

Fruits or vegetables: This group provides you with vitamins and minerals. They also contain fiber, which helps you feel full. (Fiber itself offers so many benefits that there are plenty of books written on the subject. I encourage you to read up on it!)

Healthy fats: These should be included in your diet for many reasons, one being that they help your system absorb vitamins. You can find them in olive oil, coconut oil, avocado, nuts, seeds, etc.

Again, remember this is just a simple summary of these food groups! I encourage you to go out there and learn more for yourself! With these food groups in mind, the following part of the book is broken up into three different sections: There is a section devoted to different types of vegetables, another one on how to cook different types of meat, and, last but not least, a third section on how to prepare different types of carbs/starches. I arranged the recipes in this way so that you can mix and match them for your lunches or dinners (always taking into account that you should include the four elements listed above). I want to make sure that you never feel like you are eating the same thing over and over again (unless you are into that sort of thing). Eating nutritiously does not necessarily have to be boring.

The idea came to me in this way: one day, at work, my colleagues and I were having lunch. They were mentioning how tiresome it can be to go home after work and cook a complete meal. I explained to them that it was quite simple: the centerpiece of the meal is the protein that you cook; then you just throw something in the rice cooker and steam or roast some veggies, and you have a complete meal! They were shocked and even laughed at how I simplified it. But really, nutritious, complete meals do not have to be complicated, and they can be delicious.

The next time you want to make something yummy and easy at home, come to this section of the book, and select the protein, veggie, and carb that appetizes you the most. You will be in for a delicious meal!

PROTEIN INTRODUCTION

As I mentioned in the beginning of this particular section of the book, cooking a delicious and nutritious meal does not have to be a whole ordeal. With our modern, on-the-go lifestyles, it can feel overwhelming to even think about having to cook a meal after working an eight-hour shift and sitting in traffic.

The following meat dishes are some of my favorite weeknight go-tos. After a bunch of personal trial and error, I have come up with tips to make sure they are cooked well, quickly, and deliciously. Plus, there are enough options for you to eat something different each weeknight! Go ahead and choose tonight's dish. (Save the complicated recipes for the weekends.)

Join me as we work through the different meat options. Can you find your favorite?

PERFECT CHICKEN BREAST

Back in the day, the only way you could get me to eat chicken would be if it was fried (like at Shakees—that was my fav when I was growing up!), or in caldo, or in tacos. Sometimes my mom would make us pollo guisado, usually with rice and salad, she'd pass me a chicken leg and say, "Come esto mija, so that you can have beautiful legs when you grow up." I diligently munched on those chicken legs.

That was really it. Those were the only ways I knew how to eat chicken.

Flash forward to when I met my husband. He only eats grilled chicken breast. He does not know how to eat chicken any other way. (His loss, am I right? Also, if chicken legs gave me nice legs, is chicken breast the reason he has such nice pecs? I digress.) Needless to say, since the way to my man's heart was through his stomach (hey I already had his eyes with my looks and his mind with my brains a'ight?), I learned how to make some grilled chicken breast.

I'll be honest. The first few times, it was overcooked and dry. I even thought to myself, "Ewe this is what he likes?" But, after some trial and error, I discovered the perfect way to put together a delicious and juicy grilled chicken breast. You will find that the lemon somehow makes the chicken breast tender, but never sour. My mom was shocked the first time I made chicken like this. She expected her lips to pucker, but was surprised at how flavorful and juicy the chicken was instead. This dish definitely has la Mera Mera's seal of approval. Need I say more?

Some tips before we get into it: a meat thermometer will help ensure the chicken is cooked without overcooking it. Overcooked chicken means dry chicken, and undercooked chicken is just, well, dangerous and gross. Additionally, any pan you have with grooves for grill marks will make the chicken more dynamic, with a more beautiful presentation. However, this is just optional.

MODERATE
About 30 minutes.

DIFFICULTY
MEDIUM
You got this!

SERVES **2**

Ingredients:
- 1 chicken breast
- 1 tablespoon olive oil
- 1 large lemon
- Salt and pepper, al gusto

Directions:
- Warm up a pan or comal. Once warm, add your favorite cooking oil.
- Rinse the chicken breasts and cut them in half, butterfly style (thinner chicken breasts allow for more even cooking).
- Place both halves in the warmed, oiled pan.
- Cook on high heat for three minutes. Sprinkle with salt and pepper while cooking.
- Flip the chicken, cook for three more minutes on high heat, ensuring to season this side as well.
- Lower the flame and flip the chicken again. Squeeze half a lemon onto the chicken. Cover while it cooks, for about 7 minutes.
- Flip one last time, squeeze the other lemon half onto the chicken. Cover and cook for 7 final minutes.
- Test the chicken with a meat thermometer, ensuring it is at 165 degrees.
- It should be cooked through by now. If it needs more time, allow it to reach the safe cooked temperature, checking frequently to avoid overcooking.

¡Buen provecho!

Señora Advice

*Enjoy this juicy chicken breast with a side of quinoa and some roasted broccoli! Or simply enjoy it with your favorite side dishes.

*You can use lemon pepper in place of normal pepper for more flavor!

*Works amazing sliced, with fajitas, or sliced in tacos

SIZZLING SIRLOIN

Who doesn't love some red meat once in a while? I love sirloin because it is a cut that, when prepared properly, can taste expensive. On a Valentine's Day some years ago, I decided to make filet mignon at home. I was so worried about getting it just right, that I "practiced" the recipe on some sirloin cuts about a week before. They turned out so delicious that I realized I had been sleeping on sirloin!

Besides carne asada, sirloin has become my favorite cut of meat to cook and eat at home. It is tasty and holds up in any dish. It can be seasoned to perfection and eaten alongside asparagus and a fluffy, buttery baked potato. Alternatively, you can also enjoy it alongside some quinoa with chimichurri drizzled on top of the steak to add some flavor. The same cut of meat, enjoyed with different toppings or sides, can transform into a completely different yet always tasty dish.

Finally, sirloin is a lean cut of meat. There is not a lot of fat to it, yet it still has a lot of flavor.

Do your best to buy grass-fed and organic meat, and you will have a meal that you can feel really good about—both in aspects of health and flavor.

MODERATE
About 30 minutes.

DIFFICULTY
MEDIUM
You got this!

SERVES
2

Ingredients:

- 2 sirloin fillets
- 1 tablespoon of olive oil
- 1 tablespoon of organic, grass-fed butter
- Freshly cracked pepper and sea salt, al gusto

Directions:

- Rinse the fillets and let them rest on the counter for about 30 minutes.
- After 30 minutes, rub with salt and pepper.
- At medium heat, warm up the pan. Once warm, add oil. (Using a pan with grooves for grill marks comes in handy here, presentation-wise.)
- Once the oil is warm, add the filets.
- Cook for 5 minutes, flip and then cook for 5 minutes on the other side.
- Lower the flame.
- Flip once more.
- Add the butter and proceed to bathe the sirloin in butter (get a spoon and keep spooning the butter over the meat while it cooks) for about 1 or 2 minutes.

¡Buen provecho!

Señora Advice

*Note that this recipe will have your meat cooked medium to medium-rare. If you prefer or need for it to be well done, you can preheat the oven at 400 and then finish the cooking process there for 5 to 10 minutes, depending on your desired "doneness."

*Serve it sliced to ensure the meat is cooked to your preference.

*Enjoy this sirloin with roasted potatoes and asparagus.

SECRET SALMON

Personally, salmon is my favorite fish. It has a robust flavor that comes from its fat, which, incidentally, is a healthy fat. Rich in omegas and protein, salmon can be a nutritious part of any meal.

Most people agree that white wine pairs best with fish. Pero yo digo que salmon is so flavorful that it actually holds up well with a light Pinot Noir. That is how I prefer to enjoy it with a meal. The two complement each other beautifully. Try it. I bet you'll never be able to pair salmon with white wine again.

Salmon is so rich in flavor that it can be eaten with a salad and rice, or with a woody green vegetable and potatoes. You can grill it, poach it, or steam it, but my favorite way to enjoy it is roasted.

My mom would work late once a week, and my dad and I would take the opportunity to eat salmon together. This was because, pobrecita, my mom is allergic to fish and cannot even be home when it's prepared. We'd enjoy the meal and clean well before she came back home. The salmon felt like contraband in the household! Now I live with my husband, and enjoy salmon whenever I like, which is once a week for its benefits (like omegas, for instance). Yet I still think back to those days when salmon was a precious treat. That is why I called this recipe "secret salmon."

MODERATE
30-45 minutes.

DIFFICULTY
EASY TO MEDIUM

SERVES **2**

Ingredients:

- 2 salmon fillets
- 1 tablespoon of olive oil
- 2 teaspoons of organic, grass-fed butter, melted
- Salt and pepper, al gusto
- Lemon, for garnishing on the cooked salmon
- Dried herbs (such as thyme or rosemary), optional

Directions:

- Preheat the oven to 400 degrees.
- Rinse salmon fillets.
- Place the fillets skin side down on a baking sheet lined with parchment paper.
- Drizzle olive oil, sea salt, and freshly cracked pepper onto the salmon.
- Brush a teaspoon of melted grass-fed butter on top of each filet.
- Bake for 25 minutes at 400 degrees.
- The filets should be flaky and almost crispy by the time you remove them from the oven.
- Optional: sprinkle with fresh or dried herbs like thyme or rosemary, or add garlic and onion, but remember they are not necessary for the fish to be flavorful.

¡Buen provecho!

Señora Advice
*Enjoy it with a fresh squeeze of lemon and your favorite sides, like buttery cauliflower or green beans.

CRISPY TILAPIA

I recall seeing a lot of colleagues bringing steamed tilapia and broccoli to work in meal prep containers in an effort to stay trim. And I could see why, at about only 200 calories, tilapia offers protein, vitamins, and omegas. Let's be real, though, tilapia is a mild white fish. Y, si solo lo has comido mal preparado (i.e., steamed), you may think that it's a rather flavorless fish. No worries, though, fam! I'm here to give you all the tips to make this nutrient-dense fish while still enjoying a ton of flavor.

Back in the day, I would only eat tilapia if it was breaded and fried in oil. Thankfully, I've discovered a way to make it easier on the arteries and waistline, while still being just as tasty.

My go-to method, yet again, is to roast this fish on a baking sheet lined with parchment paper. This allows me to cook with less oil, and prevents the fish from breaking up because, whenever I attempt to grill tilapia in a pan on my stovetop, it tends to crumble apart as I try to flip it. Oops! You don't have to worry about that when you roast it!

Since tilapia has such a mild flavor, you want to have fun with its seasoning. Rinse the fillets and then marinate them in a mixture of lemon juice, olive oil, melted, organic, grass-fed butter (optional), sea salt, freshly cracked pepper, and your favorite herbs. I normally throw in minced cilantro, but minced garlic and onion also go well. This fish will take any flavor you put into it, so be intentional and strategic.

MODERATE
30-45 minutes.

DIFFICULTY
MEDIUM

SERVES
2

Ingredients:

- 2 tilapia fillets
- 1 teaspoon of minced cilantro
- 1 teaspoon of fresh cracked pepper
- Sea salt, al gusto
- The juice from one lemon or lime
- Lime zest of half a lime
- 1 teaspoon of olive oil
- 1 clove of garlic, minced
- A pinch of paprika (for color)

Directions:

- Preheat the oven to 425 degrees.
- Rinse the tilapia fillets.
- Pat dry.
- In a bowl, toss tilapia filets with the minced garlic, cilantro, lime zest, pepper, salt, paprika, and olive oil. If you have time, allow them to marinate as you clean up and prepare your sides for the meal.
- Lay the filets down on a baking sheet lined with parchment paper.
- Bake for 20 to 25 minutes, until the edges are browned but not burned.
- Optional: flip over halfway through.
- Enjoy with a squeeze of lemon or lime!

¡Buen provecho!

Señora Advice

*To maximize time, prepare your side dishes while the tilapia roasts in the oven.

*Enjoy these crispy, tasty filets with your favorite sides, like a cabbage salad and white rice.

SPEEDY SHRIMP

Shrimp is low in calories and high in protein. It also contains omegas and antioxidants. However, it gets a bad rap due to being high in cholesterol. A serving size is only about seven shrimps and overeating it may not be the best idea, even with all the antioxidants and omegas it offers. It is ultimately what you are comfortable with, and you can always discuss it with your doctor for more information.

What I like about shrimp is that it is a very quick cooking protein. It takes less cooking time than any of the other proteins in this book. This is great for home cooks who want a delicious meal in a small amount of time.

Shrimp is also versatile. Put it on top of rice with a salad on the side, and you have a balanced, plated meal. You can also put some shrimp in a tortilla with salsa and chopped lettuce for soft shrimp tacos. ¡Uy, qué rico!

When shopping for shrimp, do your best to buy peeled, deveined shrimp. Peeling it and removing the spine is so much work! Why bother with all that fuss when you can already buy it prepared from the store? Additionally, before cooking it, remove the tails. That way, it is easier to eat once it's cooked, plus it's a nice, small gesture for whomever you are cooking for (including yourself).

FAST
Less than
30 minutes.

DIFFICULTY
MEDIUM

SERVES
2

Ingredients:

- 1/2 b shrimp. (Do your best to get peeled and de-veined shrimp to make your life easier.)
- 1 teaspoon of organic, grass-fed butter
- 1 tablespoon of olive oil
- 1 clove of garlic, minced
- 1 tablespoon of minced onion
- 1 pinch of lemon pepper
- 1 pinch of salt
- 2 lemons

Directions:

- Rinse the peeled and deveined shrimp.
- Mince the garlic and onion; mix them together.
- Melt the butter.
- In a bowl, add the peeled shrimp, the juice of one lemon, the minced garlic and onion, the melted butter, plus the salt and pepper. Toss them all together to coat the shrimp evenly.
- Heat a pan over medium heat. Once warm, add the olive oil.
- Add the shrimp to cook, stirring it around to ensure the butter, garlic, and onion do not burn. Do this for 5 minutes.
- Flip the shrimp over to cook the other side, for about 5 more minutes.
- Flip the shrimp one last time and reduce the heat to the lowest setting. Cover the pan to let the shrimp steam in the juices for 2 to 3 more minutes.
- Serve the shrimp and garnish with the second lemon.

¡Buen provecho!

Señora Advice

*Enjoy this over rice with salad or over a corn tortilla with cabbage slaw.

*Pairs well with a margarita.

VEGETABLES INTRODUCTION

My husband talks to me about his upbringing in El Salvador very often. As a baby, his diet consisted of breast milk and steamed vegetables fresh off the land. Life was different in El Salvador, and with a stay-at-home mom, plus a grandma and tías (who happened to live near enough to help each other with the kids), he was always well fed. No pues, wow!

I, on the other hand, was born and raised in the United States. On top of that, I had a working mother. My intention here isn't to dis' working or stay-at-home moms; I have respect for all mothers since they are the creators of life. They incarnate the spirits of their children into this world. What I am pointing out here is that, even though my mom did cook homemade food every night for dinner after a long day working at her bakery, I did not have several different women who devoted themselves to feeding me. What I had was sopitas de caja (y de lata) that I taught myself to make, bean burritos my Nana would make me, caliditos, and milk with coffee in it. (It's the only way I liked to drink milk, OK?) Needless to say, for a long time I thought vegetables were nasty. Like, a really long time. I just wasn't used to eating them. Can you relate?

As I matured, my palate became more sophisticated, and I began tasting new things mostly because el Willy encouraged and asked me to. (We've been a good influence on each other.) Thankfully, I managed to make vegetables a staple in my diet because I found out they can taste good and make me feel good. This vegetable section includes twice as much recipes as the meats and carbs section in order to give you a broader variety of options and ensure you get your vegetables every day. Let's see if you can spot your favorite vegetable.

GREEN SALAD

This salad tastes like I'm eating something indulgent when, in fact, I am just eating a salad. If you've been pregnant, you probably know that it's not uncommon to start hating some of the foods you used to love, or even the other way around. When I was in my first trimester of pregnancy, it was really hard for me to eat any vegetables. This felt a bit wrong because, now that I'm an adult, I normally love vegetables. But during those first few months of pregnancy, thanks to morning sickness, vegetables made me want to gag. This salad always came to the rescue, though! It was a sure-fire and refreshing way to nourish my body and my growing baby boy with some greens.

The limón, olive oil, and salt are all you need to make it taste good. Add red onion, tomato, and lettuce to get a satisfying crunch when you eat it as well. In addition, you can use pink Himalayan salt to add some extra minerals.

This salad will go with anything and it's a perfect side dish for steak with chimichurri, mild white fish seasoned with herbs, you name it. It's so simple and delicious, and I love it for entertaining. You can make a small portion for yourself or a big bowl for guests as an appetizer. Honestly, I can sort of eat a big bowl of this all by myself.

FAST
About 15 minutes. Chop and mix, and you are good to go!

DIFFICULTY
EASY
¡FACILÍSIMO!

SERVES
2

Ingredients:
- 1 bunch of romaine lettuce
- 2 tomatoes
- 1/2 of a red onion
- 1 tablespoon of olive oil
- 1 lemon
- 1 teaspoon of salt

Directions:
- Rinse and dry the vegetables.
- Cut the romaine lettuce into small bite size pieces.
- Cut the tomatoes into chunks.
- Cut the onion into thin strips.
- Toss in a large bowl and add olive oil, lemon, and salt. You can add more lemon for a more puckery kick.

¡Buen provecho!

Señora Advice
*You can run the lettuce through a salad spinner so that it is not too watery. If it's too watery, the salad will be hard to dress.

*This salad is so light. Pair it with a robust, flavorful steak as a refreshing and light side dish.

PERFECT ASPARAGUS

I'm going to be straight up with you. I had never eaten asparagus in my life until I met my husband. I grew up on broccoli, green beans, salads, carrots, and the like. El Willy's favorite vegetable, however, is asparagus. Once I tasted it, I was hooked. Because of this, I decided to learn to make it, so that we could eat it a few times a week for dinner. And, after some trial and error, I have figured out the easiest way to make it.

The best part of asparagus is that it accompanies poultry, beef, or fish excellently. I have cooked it to accompany filet mignon, carne asada, white fish like tilapia, or more flavorful fish like salmon. I love keeping asparagus in the fridge because it pairs well with most meals.

If you get the texture just right to where it is cooked but still has a crisp, it can satisfy even the pickiest eaters. Once, I made this for my compadres and their children when they came over. Their oldest daughter was barely three at the time. She loves trying new foods, and, once she tasted one asparagus spear, she just had to have another. She couldn't get enough of it! She looked so adorable chowing down the asparagus, and we were all so proud of her for liking her vegetables! I hope you like this recipe as much as she did.

When shopping for asparagus, I like to go for thick spears. To me, they are more satisfying. No wimpy spears here! A hack: when cutting the bottoms off, you can try to bend the spear. The hard, woody ends will snap off on their own, leaving the edible tops ready to be enjoyed.

SUPER FAST
Less than 10 minutes.

EASY
¡FACILÍSIMO!

SERVES 2

Ingredients:
- 1 bunch of asparagus
- Salt, al gusto

Directions:
- Bring salted water to boil.
- While you wait for the water to boil, rinse the asparagus and break off the woody ends.
- Once the water is at a rolling boil, gently put the asparagus spears into the water.
- Boil for 4 minutes. A timer helps here!
- After 4 minutes, turn off the stove. Remove the spears from the hot water and rinse in cold water.

Enjoy as a versatile side dish with your favorite meal.

Señora Advice
*Asparagus goes great with chicken, fish, or steak!

GREEN BEANS, AL DENTE

Green Beans are delicious. I like to steam them in boiling salted water for six minutes to get that perfect amount of doneness without any sogginess. You can certainly enjoy them roasted as well, but for this recipe, I find steamed is best.

I cannot think of green beans without recalling how my mom would put them into scrambled eggs. I'd eat them with corn tortillas and Tapatío. So bomb. With that in mind, you can make these green beans for dinner and have leftovers for breakfast the next day. As simple and easy as this recipe is, you should consider that timing is key.

When steaming green beans, watch them: you will see they develop a beautiful bright green color as they cook. It amazes me every time.

SUPER FAST
Less than
10 minutes.

DIFFICULTY
EASY
¡FACILÍSIMO!

SERVES
2

Ingredients:

- 2 cups of green beans, chopped
- Salt, al gusto

Directions:

- Bring salted water to a boil.
- While you wait for the water to boil, rinse the green beans and cut off the ends.
- Put the green beans to boil for exactly 6 minutes. (Like with asparagus, a timer is useful here.) After that, turn the heat off. Remove the green beans from the water. Rinse in cold water.
- Optional: add your favorite seasoning. I like to garnish mine with olive oil and fresh, cracked pepper.

¡Buen provecho!

Señora Advice

*Enjoy as a side dish to accompany fish or
chicken and quinoa.

ROASTED BROCCOLI

When it comes to broccoli, there are so many different ways to explore and enjoy it. Cut it finely for a salad, steam the florets, or break off some broccoli steaks to blanche or grill. My favorite way to eat it is roasted because it gets very crispy. Olive oil, salt and pepper are all you need. Also, is there anything more satisfying than a crispy crunch at dinner time?

I find that roasted broccoli can be paired with steak, chicken or fish, you name it. It can also go with rice or roasted potatoes—whatever you wish. It's a versatile side dish, and that's exactly why it's in this section!

I cannot write about roasted broccoli without thinking back to a few Thanksgivings ago. I was a newlywed and finally entrusted to bring my own dish to my family's Thanksgiving dinner. It was like an initiation to the señora club! I wanted to dazzle everyone with a variety of veggie dishes: steamed green beans, grilled peppers, and roasted broccoli. Well, as is common here in the US, the store was packed when I went shopping. Needless to say, I was frazzled by the time I finally got the ingredients. What can I say? I made a mistake and did not buy enough broccoli. It was bad. Really bad. In the end, there was like one cup of roasted broccoli for the whole family (all eighteen of us at the time). Basically, everyone ended up with one sad little broccoli floret on their plate. We were all laughing about it. But they all said it was delicious even with the tiny amount they had!

When hosting, I prefer to make broccolini over broccoli because it makes me feel fancy. Whichever one you prefer, you can prepare them in the same way. Just make sure you buy enough for your whole family or they'll end up eating just one floret each!

FAST
Less than 30 minutes.

DIFFICULTY
EASY
¡FACILÍSIMO!

SERVES
2

Ingredients:
- 2 cups of broccoli florets
- 1 tablespoon of olive oil
- Salt and pepper, al gusto

Directions:
- Preheat the oven to 400 degrees.
- Rinse the broccoli or broccolini.
- Remove any leaves.
- Chop off ends.
- In a bowl, toss with olive oil, salt, and pepper.
- Place on a baking sheet lined with parchment paper.
- Roast in the oven for 20 minutes.

¡Buen provecho!

Señora Advice
*It pairs perfectly well with steak, salmon, or chicken and your favorite glass of wine!

PEPPERS AND ONIONS
BASE (AKA FAJITA VEGETABLES)

One of my friends inspired this recipe. We were swapping meal prep tips, and she told me her favorite food to make in a large batch was sausage with peppers and onions. She said that it was even more delicious when reheated because the flavors blended together. And added that her favorite way to eat it is on top of a bed of rice. Well, after hearing her speak so enthusiastically, I had to try it for myself!

My homegirl was right. It was mouthwatering and flavorful. I couldn't get enough! I changed it up, though, because I don't like eating the same thing over and over again. I tried peppers and onions with sliced sirloin steak (much like fajitas) and sliced chicken breast. I also tried different colors of bell peppers, and even threw in a pasilla pepper every once in a while. It turns out, you can get any sort of onion and any combination of peppers along with your favorite protein, and you'll have a delicious meal.

Through some trial and error, I discovered that, if you want to add protein to the dish, the key is to cook the protein first and then add the vegetables in at the end. This ensures the vegetables will not be too soggy. I personally love that al dente crunch.

On top of being a recipe book, I want this book to be a plethora of ideas for home cooks. Sometimes, when I go to the grocery store, I find myself strolling along the aisles and thinking "What do I want to eat?" Other times, I get in a rut and feel like I repeat and cook the same things all the time. This vegetable base is so versatile and fun and a great way to eat veggies with dinner every night. Plus, who doesn't love a splash of vibrant colors on their dinner plate?

FAST
About 20 minutes.
It's a quick side dish!

DIFFICULTY
EASY TO MEDIUM

SERVES
4

Ingredients:

- 1 medium onion
- 2 bell peppers, preferably of different colors. The different colors add vibrancy to this dish.
- 1 poblano pepper
- 1 tablespoon of olive oil
- Salt and pepper, al gusto

Directions:

- Rinse and dry the vegetables.
- Cut the onion into strips.
- Cut the peppers into strips, disposing of seeds and veins.
- Warm the pan at medium heat. Once the pan is warm, add the oil.
- Once the oil is ready, after about a minute, add the peppers.
- Stir constantly for even cooking.
- Add salt and pepper and continue to stir.
- Once the onions are translucent, you are ready to enjoy!

¡Buen provecho!

Señora Advice

*When eating this with sliced chicken breast, I like to use Knorr chicken-flavored seasoning in place of salt and pepper. Once my mom tasted this hack, she was completely blown away. It got la Jefa's approval, so try it for yourself and see what you think!

*Enjoy this with fresh corn tortillas and sliced sirloin or chicken breast.

*The peppers and onion base tastes even better the next day, reheated!

CRUNCHY CABBAGE SALAD

One of the easiest ways to get me to eat vegetables is to put lime juice, salt, and chile on them. It's been this way since I was a child. One of my favorite veggie side dishes when I was growing up was my mom's cabbage salad. She would chop everything up with such care and skill. The cabbage was just thin enough to be crispy, the tomatoes were always just right (she is an expert at using them fresh, just before they become overripe), and the rábanos would stain the lemon juice with a beautiful pink color. All of the ingredients came together beautifully.

When she would make it for us, this salad typically accompanied pollo guisado and white rice. But really, this salad can be eaten with anything, in my opinion. It can accompany enchiladas, carne asada, tilapia. You get the idea.

My brother and I would typically fight over the bottom of the salad, which was extra flavorful and lemony. In the end, we would just end up sharing it. Sometimes we would even take turns sipping lime juice out of the bowl. RIP to my childhood tooth enamel, again.

I cannot make or eat this salad without thinking about my childhood. I am still in awe at how my mother managed to run a business and come home to cook us a delicious meal every weeknight. My dad's long hours at the port in the union and my mom's business provided for us. However, even though they both worked long hours, quality family time and an excellent home-cooked meal were never compromised. I hope you enjoy my own take on this salad as much as I do!

FAST
Less than 15 minutes.

DIFFICULTY
EASY
¡FACILÍSIMO!

SERVES
4

Ingredients:
- 1/2 of a cabbage
- 6 radishes
- 1 cucumber
- 1 carrot
- 1/2 of a jalapeño
- A handful of cilantro
- Lemon, salt, and olive oil
- Tomatoes, optional

Directions:
- Wash and dry the vegetables.
- Mince the cilantro.
- In a small bowl, mix olive oil, lemon juice, minced cilantro, and salt to create a simple dressing.
- Slice the jalapeño and add it to the dressing to infuse it with flavor.
- While the dressing is infusing, finely chop the cabbage.
- Cut the radishes into thin slices.
- Dice the cucumber into half-inch cubes. Optional: you can remove the cucumber seeds too.
- Grate the carrot.
- Remove the jalapeño slices from the dressing and discard them.
- In a bowl, toss the chopped vegetables with the dressing to create your salad. Mix well.

¡Buen provecho!

Señora Advice
*Enjoy this salad with grilled chicken breast and white rice for a refreshing and balanced meal!

*Another tasty option is to use this salad to garnish shrimp tacos!

CACTUS SALAD

Nopales are delicious. I have mad respect for anyone who knows how to remove the thorns. One of my tías is a master thorn-remover, and I would stare at her in awe at any carne asada as she removed thorns from the nopales, never once hurting herself, at least that I saw.

I wish I was that talented. Instead, I buy nopales in one of two ways from the carnicería: the flat paddles that are ready to go on the grill, or the bag of chopped up nopales. For today, I am going to talk about the second option.

The bag of chopped nopales is great because they are ready to use, with all the thorns removed. In that way, it saves me time and effort. However, there is still some preparation to take care of. The nopalitos must be cooked in boiling water and rinsed in cold water. You want them cooked just right, al dente. The key is to cook them just enough so they still have a crunch. After all, no one wants a mushy salad.

You can add the usual delicious ingredients, such as tomatoes, onions, cilantro, lime, and salt; you can also add chunks of avocado. Due to the different textures of nopales, avocado, and the other ingredients, this recipe makes for a delightful salad.

MODERATE
30-45 minutes.

DIFFICULTY
MEDIUM

SERVES
4

Ingredients:

- 1/2 bag of pre-cut nopalitos from the carnicería
- 2 roma tomatoes
- 1/2 of a red onion
- 1 avocado
- 1 chile pepper of your choice, both serrano or jalapeño work well
- 1 handful of cilantro
- Lemon
- Salt, al gusto

Directions:

- Bring salted water to a boil.
- Rinse the nopalitos and then place them into the boiling water. Let them cook for 15 minutes and drain. You can rinse with cold water to halt the cooking process.
- While the nopalitos cook, wash and dry the vegetables.
- Chop the onion, tomato, and avocado into equally-sized pieces, about half to one-inch pieces.
- Finely mince the cilantro leaves, removing any stems.
- Finely mince the chile pepper, removing any seeds or veins.
- In a bowl, toss the tomato, onion, cilantro, chile, avocado, and (cooked and cooled) nopalitos with lemon and salt.

Enjoy this with your favorite meal!

Señora Advice
*I love this salad with carne asada and sopita de arroz!

BUTTERY CAULIFLOWER

Cauliflower has come up. It has been turned into rice, pizza crust, and chips. Those are all delicious ways to eat it, but sometimes I just want regular cauliflower.

I like preparing it the way I am about to show you, with organic grass-fed butter. Butter can be considered a healthy fat as long as it is eaten in moderation and you choose real, organic grass-fed butter. No margarine, por los cielos, please.

The cauliflower itself has such a mild taste (that's probably why it is so versatile) that it absorbs the buttery flavor beautifully. Add some sea salt and fresh cracked pepper and you have a side dish that goes with almost anything. I especially love it with buttery salmon.

What's the key with this vegetable? Cook it slowly. You start by steaming the cauliflower with just the tiniest bit of water. Once the water evaporates, it's time to add the butter! By adding the butter later and cooking on low heat, very slowly, you can avoid burning the butter.

I prefer my veggies al dente, so you will notice that the cauliflower is cooked and has the slightest crunch. ¡Qué rico!

MODERATE
Less than 30 minutes.

DIFFICULTY
MEDIUM

SERVES **2**

Ingredients:
- 2 cups of cauliflower florets
- 2 tablespoons of organic, grass-fed butter
- Salt and pepper, al gusto

Directions:
- Cut the cauliflower into florets and rinse.
- Heat up a pot on low heat. Once warm, add just a splash of water.
- Add the chopped cauliflower to the pot and cover, allowing it to steam.
- Season with salt and pepper.
- Check on it periodically, and stir.
- After about 10 minutes, add the butter.
- Stir to melt the butter and then cover for 5 more minutes.

¡Buen provecho!

Señora Advice
*This cauliflower is a perfect accompaniment to salmon.

CALABACITAS, DOS GENERACIONES

MODERATE
Over 30 minutes. Patience will provide a tasty dish.

DIFFICULTY
MEDIUM

SERVES

As I write this, I am five months pregnant with my first child, a baby boy who I am already obsessed with and extremely eager to meet. My mom has come over to help me around the house while I focus on working and bed rest. As I write this particular recipe, she is making it for me to satisfy an antojito. As you can imagine, the house smells amazing.

This recipe is a great way for picky eaters to get in their veggies. The corn adds a sweet crunch, the melted cheese adds gooey goodness, and the spicy tomato juice/sauce helps to tie all the flavors together. You steam the calabacitas just right, and you have a comforting and savory dish packed with nutrients!

You can enjoy this on top of white rice for a meatless meal, pair it with chicken or steak, or enjoy it alone as a very light meal or snack. This dish is very versatile, which is why it is important for me to share it with you. This book is all about easy versatility, and making yummy food to nourish your body and soul while being practical and time-conscious.

I call this recipe Calabacitas Dos Generaciones, because it is originally my mom's recipe. She makes it with tomato sauce and chopped zucchini. I prefer to make it with salsa roja and zoodles. You will see the recipe in this book is a bit of a hybrid. However you decide to make it, I promise this will be a warm and delicious comfort food! And a great way to get in some yummy veggies.

Ingredients:

- 2 zucchinis (summer squashes work as well)
- 1/2 of an onion
- Canned tomato sauce or leftover salsa roja, about one cup
- 1 cup of grated cheese
- 1 tablespoon of olive oil
- 1 cup of canned corn
- Salt and pepper, al gusto
- Mrs. Dash Seasoning, al gusto

Directions:

- Wash, dry, and chop the squash and onion.
- Warm a pan to medium heat and add some olive oil.
- As the oil warms, add the onion to infuse the oil with flavor.
- After a few minutes, when the onion is just starting to turn translucent, stir in the squash and corn. Season with salt, pepper, and Mrs. Dash.
- Lower the heat to a simmer and cover the pot for about ten minutes, allowing the squash to steam.
- While the squash steams, grate the cheese.
- Once the squash starts to turn translucent, add the tomato sauce. Stir, so that all the flavors blend together.
- Watch closely and stir consistently. Once the tomato sauce has bubbled and you see that the squash has a softer, cooked texture, stir well, again. You want to really make sure to evenly distribute the saucy flavors.
- Turn off the heat. Sprinkle the cheese on top, and cover the pot again. The residual heat will melt the cheese perfectly without burning it.

¡Buen provecho!

Señora Advice
*Enjoy this on top of rice with pollo guisado.
*You can use zoodles here as well.
*Fresh cracked pepper offers the best flavor!

LAZY VEGGIE TRAY

So far, you have read all about cooking veggies: how to steam, roast, and sauté them. You have also learned how to season them. By now, you should be a pro at cooking vegetables. You need that level of confidence to make this veggie tray.

When I was learning to cook, I remember how accomplished I felt when I made something without a list or recipe. I simply gathered the ingredients from my fridge and pantry and went to town! With this veggie tray, I want you to feel the same way. Which vegetables are your favorite? All you have to do is rinse them, pat them dry, chop them up and toss them with olive oil, salt, and cracked pepper. Put them into the oven at 400 degrees for 20 minutes, and, boom, you have a side dish!

That's it. It's that simple. Remember, I am all about honoring traditions and our ancestors, but I am also into fitting cooking into my busy schedule! I love roasting my dinner because I can set it and forget it. In today's modern world, there is so much to do—working, working out, cooking, cleaning, spending time with family, resting, and getting in ten hours of mindlessly scrolling through your IG with Netflix on in the background. No, but really! If you can set it and forget it, why not?

MEDIUM
About 30 minutes.

DIFFICULTY
EASY TO MEDIUM

SERVES 2

Ingredients:

- 2 cups, veggies of your choice. I use whatever is in my fridge! Onions, squash, green beans, and the like, all work well. Adding more color makes dishes more fun, so don't be afraid to experiment!
- 1 or 2 tablespoons of olive oil
- Salt and pepper, al gusto

Directions:

- Preheat the oven to 400 degrees.
- Wash and dry the vegetables.
- Chop them up to your preference.
- In a large bowl, toss the chopped vegetables with oil and seasonings.
- Place the vegetables on a lined baking sheet.
- Roast for 20 to 25 minutes, until you see the edges brown to a crisp without burning.

Enjoy this as a side dish with whatever you like! This is your creation.

Señora Advice
*Watch those veggies for the last 5 minutes. That is when the difference between burning and crisping occurs.

STARCHES INTRODUCTION

As a Hispanic-American, I deal with a lot of duality in my identity. I was born and raised in the USA with Salvadorian and Mexican blood running through my veins. I am a Latina who loves the traditions of her culture and also lives a modern lifestyle. I am a daughter and, by the time this is published, a mother. Yes, I am no stranger to duality.

Why am I talking about duality here? This section is devoted to recipes of a variety of carbs and starches, and, as we all know, these tend to be quite controversial: some people support them, and some others don't. But, hear me out: duality can exist in how we view our food choices too. In our Latin culture, carbs are central to our meals: tortillas, rice, beans, corn, etc. Yet, in US diet culture, carbs are frowned upon. (I'm sure most of us can think of a few different fad diets off the top of our heads that discourage the consumption of carbs.)

So, as a US-based Latina, where do I find myself in the middle of all this info about carbs? I am not a nutritionist by any means, but I have experimented with some of those low-carb diets, and I've also gone the route of eating carbs like a free for all. Neither one made me feel my best. Rather, finding the right balance for me is what makes me feel full and healthy. I try not to overeat carbs, but I avoid cutting them out completely. Carbs can make a person feel satisfied and energized too; the secret lies in how you eat them. I encourage you to find the right balance for yourself!

In this section, you will find a few different recipes to choose from when cooking your own staches at home. It is my hope that there is something for everyone. Remember that beans, potatoes, and quinoa are also nutrient dense. These are not refined carbs like white pasta and white bread, so go ahead and enjoy them because these carbs offer your mind, body, and spirit a healthy and delicious eating experience that will remind you of your heritage while nourishing your body.

CLASSIC CASAMIENTO

Casamiento is a Salvi staple. You can eat it for breakfast, lunch, or dinner with some queso fresco on top. Pues wow, it's the ultimate comfort food.

The great thing about casamiento is that you can make it with leftover black beans and leftover white rice. You can also make it with canned black beans and rice cooker rice. My mom says that's not real casamiento. I tell her that I'm a working woman who finds and uses kitchen hacks whenever I can.

Mix the black beans and white rice together and freeze your casamiento so that you always have a side dish a mano. It defrosts quickly on the stovetop, so it is great for meal prepping. Some Sundays I play housewife and bust down in the kitchen, freezing things ahead of time that will come in handy on hectic days. Other Sundays, I can't be bothered to have a whole production of meal prepping in my kitchen and opt to spend my day in a horizontal position on the couch. It's called balance, OK?

However you decide to make casamiento, I hope you enjoy it! Remember that seasoning is everything. If you're Salvadorian, I bet this dish is a comfort food for you, like it is for me. If you're not Salvadorian, igual te lo comes and enjoy every bite so you can see what the hype is about. Think of me and your other Salvi friends when you do so.

FAST
About 15 minutes.

DIFFICULTY
EASY

SERVES
2

Ingredients:

- 1 cup of cooked black beans. Leftovers work great for this recipe.
- 1 cup of cooked rice. Leftover rice works great here too.
- Knorr seasoning. I use a teaspoon. My suegra uses a tablespoon. It's your choice!
- 1 tablespoon of olive oil

Directions:

- Warm a pan on medium heat. Once warm, add the olive oil.
- After about a minute, add in the rice and beans.
- Sprinkle the Knorr seasoning on top.
- Stir the rice and beans together in the pan. Fold them into each other.
- Keep an eye on this so it does not burn.
- You will see the rice pick up color from the beans. This indicates they are mixing well together.
- Once the rice and beans are mixed evenly and are warmed thoroughly, you are ready to enjoy!

¡Buen provecho!

Señora Advice
*Enjoy with pico de gallo and queso fresco on top.
*Enjoy at breakfast, accompanied by fried plantains or fried eggs.
*Enjoy at lunch or dinner with some chicken and chayotes.
*It also pairs well with a Pilsner beer!

LA DOÑITA'S QUINOA

This is not a vegetarian cookbook, but for those of you looking for alternative protein sources, quinoa is an excellent choice. This is because it is a complete protein. As a matter of fact, it is a seed that is eaten as a grain. Quinoa is so good for our bodies that it is considered a superfood. It contains protein, folate, magnesium, and fiber; it has a nutty taste and pairs well with lots of dishes. The key is to make sure it does not get too soggy when preparing it.

The biggest tip I can share is to make quinoa in a rice cooker. It is ridiculously easy and ensures that it will come out right every time. Additionally, use chicken broth instead of water to really give it some good flavor. Finally, throw some frozen veggies in there to mix it up. Most of the time, I throw in chopped-up leftover green beans.

As I mentioned a few recipes ago, my husband's best friend is SalviMex like me. His mother is the one who gave me the advice to make quinoa this way. What I love about la doñita is that she keeps it real! She agrees that, while quinoa is super nutritious, it can be so boring if not prepared correctly. La doñita is the one who gave me the tips to cook it with chicken broth and some chopped veggies to give it flavor and life. After all, who says eating healthy superfoods has to be boring? We just have to make tiny tweaks to our everyday diets to make it enjoyable, and we will be on our way to living a nutritious lifestyle.

The first few times I tried quinoa, I thought it was soggy, bland, and straight-up gross. Gotta be honest, right? But my señora friend changed my mind. With her tips, I was able to prepare quinoa that was tasty and satisfying. I hope these tips help you as much as they helped me!

FAIRLY FAST
About 30 minutes. Set it and forget it.

DIFFICULTY
EASY TO MEDIUM

SERVES 4

Ingredients:
- 1 cup of quinoa
- 1 cup of green beans (fresh, frozen, or canned)
- 2 cups of chicken broth
- Salt, al gusto

Directions:
- Rinse the quinoa.
- Rinse the green beans.
- Put the quinoa, green beans, broth, and salt into the rice cooker.
- Cook on the normal rice cooker setting.

¡Buen provecho!

Señora Advice
*I set it and forget it. For instance, while it cooks, I start on my meat and veggies.
*Once cooked, set aside any leftover quinoa in a glass container with an airtight lid. The quinoa will keep well in the fridge for up to a week!

ROASTED POTATOES

Potatoes are yummy in almost any way you have them: French fries, hash browns, baked potato, mashed potatoes. There could probably even be a whole cookbook on potatoes alone. Right now, though, I want to talk about my latest obsession with roasted potatoes. Life hack: you can have them for breakfast, lunch, or dinner—honestly! Whenever you decide to eat them, they are absolutely delicious. Make them just right, and they will be crispy on the outside and fluffy on the inside.

After rinsing and chopping, you can put a big batch into the oven. This is great if you are hosting a large crowd, para que abunde la comida. I remember one night when all of el Willy's siblings came over to dinner at the last minute. It was hilarious. It all started with my concuño, who wanted to come over to just hang out. His partner, my cuñada, decided to join too. Then my husband's little brother, other sister, and her husband said, well, we want to join too! I went from expecting a couple of guests to hosting/feeding about eight adults, including myself and el Willy. This was when roasted potatoes came to the rescue. It's easy to make a big batch without inconveniencing yourself.

My husband and I love that his siblings and my siblings know they can come over to eat and drink good stuff when they're here. He and I are both very social and love being around our loved ones, and this recipe comes to the rescue whenever I want to feed our large families. And they are large! He is the oldest of four and I am the youngest of five.

Whether you have a lot of people to feed or just love potatoes, chop them, toss them with olive oil, salt, and pepper, and roast them at 425 degrees for 45 minutes. I promise you'll love it and it'll be a crowd-pleaser too!

MODERATE
Over 45 minutes. But you can set it and forget it!

DIFFICULTY
EASY TO MEDIUM

SERVES 2

Ingredients:
- 2 cups baby potatoes or fingerling potatoes
- 2 tablespoons of olive oil
- Salt and pepper, al gusto

Directions:
- Preheat the oven to 425 degrees.
- Wash and dry the potatoes.
- Cut the potatoes into evenly, bite-size pieces. No need to peel them!
- In a large bowl, toss the potatoes with olive oil, salt, and pepper.
- Place the potatoes on a lined baking sheet.
- Roast for 45 minutes.

¡Buen provecho!

Señora Advice
Enjoy dipped in ketchup mixed with Tapatío or with some homemade salsa drizzled on top!

SOPITA DE ARROZ

Is there a particular dish or food that you thought you could never, ever learn to cook? For me it was sopita de arroz, also known as Mexican fried rice or Spanish rice. I was always impressed by the way my mom and tías would bust it out. It looked effortless, fluffy, and full of flavor. The rice was never soggy, even though it soaked up all the tomato juice and chicken broth. Meanwhile, I could barely figure out plain white rice. Seriously, rice of all sorts confused me, but Mexican fried rice intimidated me the most. However, it is a traditional dish I cannot live without. Easter Sunday or a regular carne asada are not the same without this Mexican fried rice side dish.

I wish I could tell you that I got it right the first time, or even the fifth or sixth time. I also wish I could tell you that when I failed, I immediately got back on the horse. What I can tell you, though, is that every time I failed at it, I learned a new hack.

Rice finally comes easy to me now that I am an emotionally mature home cook. I feel like a boss señora when I show up to a reunion with my version of Mexican fried rice. I also feel proud to honor a recipe that was passed down from my grandmother to my mother and aunts, and then to me.

I hope one day my future granddaughter, who does not exist yet but who I already love so much, makes this rice, and it fills her with the same wonder with which it fills me. I hope you too feel as proud when you cook this recipe perfectly. Enjoy as you bite into this saucy rice that is not quite a sopita but almost like a hug on a cold day!

MODERATE
Over 45 minutes. Patience will come in handy here.

DIFFICULTY SEÑORA LEVEL

SERVES 4

Ingredients:

- 1 cup of rice
- About 2 cups of water
- 1/2 cup of tomato sauce
- 1/4 of an onion
- 1 tablespoon of Knorr seasoning
- Grapeseed oil, enough to cover your pan

Directions:

- Rinse the rice.
- Heat a pan. Add grapeseed oil, enough to cover it.
- Add 1/4 of an onion to infuse the oil with the flavor of the onion. (You will remove this before serving.)
- Add the rice to fry.
- Stir until it begins to bunch together.
- Add one tablespoon of Knorr chicken-flavored seasoning, and stir in well.
- Lower the heat to simmer.
- Add 1/2 cup tomato sauce and enough water to cover the rice leaving one inch of water over the rice. (It could be a little more or a little less than 2 cups, depending on your pan size.) Stir.
- Check on the rice about every ten minutes to ensure even cooking.
- Once the water has evaporated, make sure the rice is not sticking to the bottom or edges. (Do not over-stir during these steps.)
- Add a tiny bit of water if rice is sticking to the pan. The rice is ready when it looks fluffy!

¡Buen provecho!

Señora Advice
*Enjoy this rice with chicken breast or carne asada and a side salad.

NANA'S BEANS

In my home, you will often find different types of beans. I keep organic canned black beans, pinto beans, and garbanzo beans in my pantry. At any given time, I may freeze or refrigerate black beans or pinto beans, the latter whole or mashed. But, out of all the types of beans, mashed pinto beans are my absolute favorite because they remind me of my Nana.

In my family, my Nana was revered for being an amazing home cook, and guess what was her most popular recipe? Her beans, of course. You could always count on my Nana to have mashed pinto beans at her house in case her children and grandchildren stopped by. She always served them with a flour tortilla, and, if she had just come back from Sonora, she would use the flour tortillas from there. I buy them too every time I visit. These tortillas are so special because they are buttery and paper thin. A lot of us in the family agree—Sonora-style flour tortillas and Nana's Beans are simply made for each other.

Though I cannot make this dish as well as my beloved Nana did, I try my best every time and think of her when I enjoy them. I have so many lovely memories about my Nana! I spent a lot of time in her home, which always smelled of warm Mexican cooking and Suavitel fabric softener. As a little girl, I would eat these beans while drawing little houses or flowers for her. Sometimes, we would sing "Over the Rainbow," from the Wizard of Oz. It was my favorite movie as a girl, and, coincidentally, she loved it as a girl too. I would sing in English, and she would sing it in Spanish.

Other times, she'd prepare me a bean burrito after going on one of our walks. Almost every time I visited her, we would go on a walk together, and if we ran into her neighbors, she would say, "Aquí estoy con mi nieta Bernie. Ella es la más chiquita de todos." She'd boast to them that I was the youngest of all her grandchildren. Out of all twenty-five or so of her grandchildren, I am actually the second youngest. I think she liked to introduce me as "the youngest" to her friends because it was her way of expressing, in a few short words, the cariño she felt for me; or maybe it was her way of saying what a big baby I was, because I may not have been her youngest grandchild, but I sure acted like it, especially around her!

I will now share some of my Nana's secrets with you. Feel free to mash the beans by hand, use an immersion blender, or throw them into your blender. My Nana used all of these techniques. It is your call depending on your comfort level and the tools you have. I personally use my bullet blender and pulse a few times. I prefer this over manually mashing to protect my hands long term. For gooey comfort and to thicken the beans, add Monterey cheese. Finally, add jalapeño for just the right kick.

Regardless of how you choose to make these beans, I hope you enjoy them. In my case, I will be thinking about my Nana and our shared memories every time I eat this dish.

MODERATE
Over 30 minutes.

DIFFICULTY
MEDIUM

SERVES 4

Ingredients:

- 2 cups of cooked pinto beans
- 1 cup of shredded Monterey Jack cheese
- 1 fresh jalapeño pepper
  (or a few slices from a can)
- 1 tablespoon of vegetable oil
  (grapeseed works great here)

Directions:

- Rinse and chop the chile peppers, removing the stem and seeds.
- Put the beans and chopped peppers into your blender and blend to your preference.
- Warm a pan on medium heat. Once warm, add the oil.
- After about a minute, slowly and gently pour the mixture into the pan. Stir constantly.
- Allow the beans to heat up. You will see them bubble up. Once they are bubbling around all over, lower the heat to medium/low or low.
- Add the shredded cheese. Continue to constantly stir and fold in the cheese. You want to evenly distribute the cheese throughout!
- Once the cheese is melted, you are ready to enjoy the beans!

¡Buen provecho!

Señora Advice
* You can enjoy these beans as a base in sopes or tostadas.
* Try them inside pupusas.
* Enjoy them as a side dish to accompany carne asada and pico de gallo.
* You can also simply enjoy them inside a tortilla as a bean burrito snack, but try not to make them overly runny in the blender or they will spill out of the burritos too easily!

PLATOS COMPLETOS INTRODUCTION

By now, you should be feeling totally confident in the kitchen. You probably have a stash of salsas, mastered breakfast on the go, and prepared easy and nutritious weeknight dinners. I am also almost certain you have a favorite cocktail and snack!

Now we are going to change gears a little bit. The prior recipes were all designed for a Latinx person on the go who wants to efficiently enjoy the flavors of their heritage with modern and healthy hacks. No fluff. No frills.

However, if you really feel like devoting yourself to making more complex dishes, there are plenty of recipes from our culture that do require time, patience, and care. You know what I mean: what is Christmas without tamales? What is New Year's Day without panes con pollo? How could I ever make it through Lent without some chiles rellenos or mariscos?

That's where this section comes in: it contains recipes that require more work and, thus, more time. Most of them are meals I would enjoy on a weekend, and not necessarily a weeknight. (I could not imagine making tamales on a Monday night after work!) Don't get me wrong, you can absolutely enjoy a dish from this section on a Wednesday night if you actually have enough time, especially once you've gotten your groove in the kitchen. Think of caldos: they make for a great weeknight recalentado. But the truth is, nowadays, most people—including myself—arrive home after a long day of work and do not have the time or energy to cook complex dishes.

What all these recipes have in common is that they are complete meals that can be enjoyed on special occasions with loved ones or during a relaxing day at home with yourself. So, if you want to "get your señora on" and throw down in the kitchen, then join me as we review these recipes that are so significant in our culture!

I personally cannot cook these dishes without thinking of the people in my life who were, and are, so gifted at cooking. In fact, every time I make one of these recipes, I cannot help but feel accomplished. I wonder if my Nanas Isabel and Lupita would be proud of me. I know my mom certainly is. I remember the first time she saw me cook one of these platos completos on my own. She said: "Wow! Ya ni me necesitas, mija." As is that could ever be true!

FAST
Less than 30 minutes.
You just have to reheat
and assemble

DIFFICULTY
SUPER EASY

SERVES **4**

WEEKNIGHT TOSTADAS

Have you ever heard the joke about how all Mexican recipes are the same ingredients assembled in different ways? Tacos, tostadas, sopes, etc. It's meat and beans with salsa on top of some type of corn tortilla. It should come as no surprise, therefore, that I love tacos, taquitos, sopes, and tostadas all the same. Although they all share similar ingredients, let's be honest, they are all special in their own way. A sope offers the distinctive comfort of fried dough, which is so fluffy and crispy at the same time; tacos fritos or taquitos made at home with corn tortillas carry their own charm as the tortilla goes from being soft to crunchy; and, a tostada? Well, that's in a whole category on its own!

For this recipe, you can use store-bought tostadas or put some tortillas in the oven until they are crispy. I won't judge you for using store-bought tostada shells as a base. Additionally, you can use refried beans, leftover chicken breast or carne asada (chopped up and reheated), and whatever salsa is in your fridge. This way, you can create an entire meal from a variety of ingredients, in a flash. This is why I call this recipe weeknight tostadas. With these tostadas, you can enjoy leftovers that do not necessarily need to feel like leftovers.

If you find yourself in the mood to throw down in the kitchen, then I recommend taking the time to crisp up some tortillas in the oven. Once they are ready and a bit cooled, you can paint on the mashed beans, which will act as a paste to which the other ingredients will securely cling to. Top with the meat, salsa, lettuce, and queso fresco, and you will have a meal that is so satisfying. And it's so photographable too! Note: you may find a hipster calling this an "open-faced taco." Ignore them over the crunches as you chow down on your creation.

Ingredients:

- 16 tostada pre-made shells (Guerrero brand works great)
- 2 cups of leftover beans (like Nana's Beans), reheated
- 2 cups of leftover chopped meat or chicken breast, reheated
- 2 cups of finely cut lettuce
- About 1 1/2 cups of pico de gallo
- 1 cup of crumbled or grated queso fresco

Directions:

- Slather warmed beans onto the toasted ortilla/tostada.
- Spoon on meat and spread across evenly.
- Follow with lettuce, ensuring to cover evenly.
- Garnish with salsa of your choice and cheese.

¡Buen provecho!

Señora Advice

*If you have time to toast your own tortillas, you can preheat an oven to 400 degrees and line a baking sheet with parchment paper. Spray each side of your tortilla with cooking spray and cook each side for about 5 minutes or until they get a beautiful golden color. They should be crispy and firm enough to hold all your toppings!

*Don't like the oven? My suegra is a master of crisping up tortillas in the toaster oven! If you have a toaster oven, experiment with the settings and toast until golden.

*You can use any kind of meat as a base: leftover carne asada, leftover chicken or carne molida. You can also go meatless and simply enjoy bean tostadas!

MONCHI'S MEXICAN SHRIMP COCKTAIL

Growing up in my childhood home, we did not eat much fish. La Mera Mera, aka my mama, is terribly allergic to fish, pobrecita. She is allergic to all seafood, as a matter of fact. Even the smell gets to her (she doesn't even like the beach) so it was very rare that we would cook seafood at home. In fact, when we are all out at a restaurant, whoever sits next to her does not order a seafood dish out of respect.

The thing is, Monchi, aka my dad, and I love seafood! Yet, it felt like contraband at home. (Remember the secret salmon?) Hence, whenever la Mera Mera would work late, Monchi and I would sometimes go to a restaurant together, just the two of us. We would order salmon, or shrimp cocktail, or ceviche, you name it. It made for really awesome quality time between us.

A great memory I cherish takes me back to when I was little: Monchi would make me a shrimp cocktail every year for my birthday parties. It was an extra special treat. And, let me tell you, it was delicious! Now, I don't know if it tasted good because I only ate it on very special occasions, or because he made it with so much love, or because Monchi is a low-key master chef. Maybe his shrimp cocktail is delicious for all those reasons.

Since seafood was so coveted in my home, I'd jokingly tell my mom that I would make seafood every night once I moved out of the house. But, shortly after I moved out, I developed an allergy to shrimp. You cannot make this up! (Really, shrimp? Why did you gotta play me like that?) I was twenty-five. My mom told me, yup, that's around the age my allergy developed. Buena suerte mija.

I may not be able to enjoy shrimp like I used to, but I still think fondly of my dad's shrimp cocktails. So, go ahead and enjoy this tasty recipe for me!

By the way, if you have never had a Mexican shrimp cocktail, it is a lot like gazpacho; it is served cold. Perfect for a summer day!

FAST
About 30 minutes.

DIFFICULTY
EASY
¡FACILÍSIMO!

SERVES 6

Ingredients:

- 1 lb bag of pre-cooked shrimp
- Chilled tomato juice like V8 or Clamato, 32 oz bottle
- Canned vegetables like corn, carrots, and peas, 1/3 can of each should do it.
- 1/2 of an onion, chopped
- 1 or 2 garlic cloves, minced
- 1 cup diced cucumber
- 1 avocado, diced
- 1 handful of cilantro leaves (no stems), minced
- 1/2 cup of lime juice

Directions:

- Rinse the shrimp and remove the veins and tails. You can buy pre-cooked shrimp that does not have veins or tails and save time.
- Optional: Boil the shrimp for 5 to 10 minutes and allow it to cool while you prepare the rest of the recipe. Even though the shrimp is pre-cooked, boiling it brings out a tender and more enjoyable texture.
- Open the cans of vegetables and rinse well.
- In a large bowl, pour in the V8 tomato juice.
- Add in the shrimp, vegetables, and lime juice. Stir.
- Chill for at least an hour before serving.

¡Buen provecho!

Señora Advice
* Enjoy with tostadas or crackers on the side.
* Garnish with more lime and add Tapatío for the best experience. Valentina works great too!

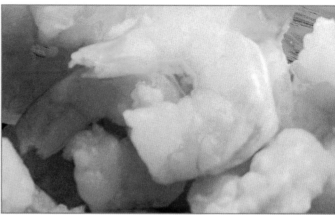

SOPITA DE QUESO

MODERATE
30-45 minutes.

DIFFICULTY
EASY TO MEDIUM

SERVES
2

My sweet Nana Isabel called this recipe her sopita de queso. I call it Mexican mac and cheese. However you call it, it is my favorite recipe of hers! (Yes, unbelievably, I love it even more than her famed frijoles.) As I've mentioned, my Nana is my grandmother on my father's side. Like a true matriarch, she welcomed everyone into her home and everyone called her Nana out of respect.

I vividly remember when she taught one of my tías on my mom's side this recipe. I was a young child, always curious, and I was in the middle between my tía and Nana throughout the entire lesson. In a way, you can say this was one of the first recipes I learned, even if it was indirectly. Now, as an adult, I am so grateful I butted in, not only because of what I learned, but also because it's one of my most cherished memories of my Nana.

My Nana passed away when I was only seventeen years old. As a teenager, I was not interested in cooking. I mourn over not learning her recipes directly from her. However, she managed to teach so many family members her recipes that they continue to be passed on from relative to relative. These recipes, these sacred treasures, live in all of us.

There is something so comforting about this sopita de queso! Maybe it's because it was my favorite of my Nana's, or maybe it's because it was a recipe I saw her teach. Either way, I love to enjoy it like comfort food on cold days. Whenever I eat it, I recall my Nana, who continues to be the family's matriarch in spirit. I dedicate this particular recipe and so many other things to my Nana, all the way up to heaven.

Ingredients:

- 3 cups of tomato sauce
- 2 cups of pasta, raw. Macaroni works great, but shells are my favorite.
- 1 cup of Monterey Jack cheese, shredded.
- 1 cup of sharp cheddar cheese, shredded.
- 1 onion
- 1 teaspoon chiltepines, crushed (red pepper flakes work too if you cannot find chiltepines)

Directions:

- Cook pasta according to cooking instructions and drain. Set it aside.
- In a saucepan, begin to warm the tomato sauce.
- Cut the onion in half removing the skin, and put it in the tomato sauce to infuse it with flavor.
- Stir in the grated cheese until it melts.
- Remove onion.
- Once the cheese and tomato sauce have combined to the desired saucy consistency, add in the cooked pasta.
- Stir in crushed chiltepines.

¡Buen provecho!

MY SUEGRITA'S SALPICÓN

MODERATE
Over 45 minutes.

DIFFICULTY
EASY
¡FACILÍSIMO!

SERVES 4

I had never had salpicón until I started dating el Willy. When we first started dating, we went to visit his parents for dinner at their home and my suegra lovingly made us some salpicón. For me, it was love at first bite. I was amazed at this dish!

If you've never had salpicón, consider it a Salvadorian minced meat dish. It is enjoyed cold, with a squeeze of lime, and plated over warm rice. It is quite refreshing. My personal favorite part of eating salpicón is squeezing lime juice all over it. (I really love sour stuff, remember?)

It may seem like a simple dish, but there is beauty in its simplicity. The onion adds just the right amount of kick, the radish makes for a refreshing crunch, and the mint explodes with fragrant flavor. The lime and salt come together so deliciously! As I write this, I am nearing the end of my second trimester of pregnancy, and, let's just say, as soon as I finish writing this recipe, I will make some Salvi salpicón, suegra style.

I am so grateful to my sweet suegra for teaching me this recipe. Seriously, not to brag about what I married into, but there's no other way to put it, my suegra makes some delicious salpicón. I want everyone to try this recipe! So, here it is. I hope that it brings you the same joy and wonder that it brought me.

Ingredients:

- 1/2 lb of beef (I ask the carnicero for meat like for beef stew)
- Radishes, one handful
- 1/2 of an onion
- 1 to 2 garlic cloves
- Mint leaves. (I add a pinch. My suegra adds a handful. It just depends on how much mint flavor you like!)
- Salt and pepper, al gusto
- Lime to garnish

Directions:

- Slow cook the beef in boiling salted water. You can add some garlic cloves to the broth to infuse it with flavor. (Once cooked, you can save the broth for later to make noodle soup!)
- Allow time for the meat to cool.
- As it cools, wash all the vegetables.
- Cut the onion and radishes into fourths and put individual mint leaves (no stems!) into the processor. Pulse a few times until you have a beautiful minced medley. (You can chop them with your hands or use a food processor. I prefer a food processor because it's easier on your hands long term. You can also use a grater.)
- Once the vegetables have the desired texture and size, put them to the side.
- In a food processor, add a little bit of cooled meat at a time to mince it. Do not add too much at once as it may become mushy, or it will not get chopped finely enough. And we want a beef mince here. That is the word of the day when making this recipe, mince!
- Once the meat is finely chopped, you can put it in a large bowl.
- Add the vegetables and mix everything together with your hands.
- Season with salt and pepper.

¡Buen provecho!

CALDO DE POLLO, BERNIE STYLE

Did your mom or grandma ever make caldo on the hottest days of summer? Mine did! Many times. Very frequently, in fact! I would come home to see my mom hovering around a simmering pot, and I would groan. My brother would laugh and crack jokes about it. However, by the time we all sat together to eat as a family, all of us were slurping up the caldo and enjoying every drop. Extra lime in mine with just a touch of Tapatío.

Now that I am older, I constantly see memes all over the internet and can tell I wasn't the only one! It seemed like every Latina mother made caldo on hot days. Why? It's one of the many mysteries of our culture. Are our moms the ultimate pranksters? Does the broth offer extra electrolytes on hot days? Or is it just easier to put soup to cook and forget about it? After all, who wants to be cooking in a hot kitchen in the middle of summer after working all day? It could be a combination of some or all of these factors or even many unknown others. We'll probably never know. What I do know is that I can't wait to make caldo on a hot summer day for my own kids one day. When that time comes, I will not do it only for the nutrients, but also for a good laugh.

Jokes and Latin mysteries aside, caldos are my go-to. A friend of mine once called it lazy cooking. I call it "working woman cooking." Caldo will appeal to the working home cook for many reasons. Take this example: last night, I made a pot of caldo, and once the soup was going, I was able to go wash my hair. Multi-tasking master right here! Additionally, my husband often times does not eat any recalentados (leftovers), except for caldo! We both agree it tastes better the next day. The fact that you can boil it again when you reheat it will satisfy any qualms of picky eaters who are hesitant about leftovers. Even if you are not a picky eater, this flavor factor is a game-changer if you are into meal prepping.

On top of being easy to make, there is something so comforting about caldo. It is warm and soothing and, like a nurturing matriarch, resourceful and adaptable.

Once you get the hang of this recipe, use any vegetables you'd like in the soup. I could probably eat caldo every night and not get tired of it because the ingredients are so easy to change up. And if that is not enough to make you love caldo, then let me tell you this, it can be fairly easy to make on a budget.

Now that I laid out all the reasons why caldo is amazing and beneficial, let's dive right into the recipe.

LONG
Over an hour. Indulge in a sheet mask while you wait!

DIFFICULTY
MEDIUM
but once you get things going, you can set it and forget it!

SERVES **6**

Ingredients:

- 4 to 6 chicken legs (the chicken leg bones make for a rich bone broth!)
- 1 chayote
- 1 squash
- 1 onion
- 2 or 3 garlic cloves
- 1 bell pepper
- 1 carrot
- 1 or 2 celery stalks
- Noodles of your choice (I love lentil or chickpea noodles for extra nutrients)
- 1 tablespoon of apple cider vinegar
- 1 tablespoon of pink Himalayan salt or Knorr chicken seasoning
- 1 tablespoon of olive oil
- 1 cup leftover salsa, optional

Directions:

- Wash all the vegetables.
- Finely chop the onion, carrots, and celery. Mince the garlic.
- Heat your large soup pot over medium heat and add the tablespoon of olive oil.
- Sauté the onion, garlic, carrots, and celery until fragrant. Lower the flame once fragrant, and be careful not to burn any of it. This is your soup starter mix.
- Once the onions and garlic are translucent, add filtered water. This will become your broth. Add salt (or Knorr chicken seasoning) and bring the water to a boil.
- In another, separate pot, bring water to a boil. Once boiling, add the chicken legs for just 2 minutes. Remove them from the pot and throw out the water. This will remove any impurities from the bones. Add the "cleaned" chicken legs to your soup base, which should be boiling by now.
- The chicken legs will require about 15 minutes to cook through. Add apple cider vinegar here to help pull minerals from the bones.
- While the chicken legs are cooking, chop up the remainder of the vegetables. (I personally love to use the "zoodler" for my squash.)
- Add the vegetables to the broth after the chicken has had a chance to cook for 15 minutes.
- While the vegetables cook, break your noodles into one or two-inch pieces and toast them on a comal. This step is totally worth it, because toasting the noodles gives them so much flavor!
- Allow the vegetables to cook for 15 minutes, and then add the noodles and cook them for another 10 minutes.
- While the noodles are cooking, you can remove the chicken legs, shred the meat, dispose of the bone and add the shredded chicken back into the soup. This extra step makes eating the soup more pleasant as there won't be any bones to gnaw on.
- At this time, if you have any salsa in your fridge, you have the option to stir it into your boiling pot.

¡Buen provecho!

Señora Advice
* Enjoy this chicken noodle soup with tortillas and queso on the side.
* You can garnish the soup itself with a squeeze of lemon, a dash of Tajín and, perhaps the decoration of a cilantro leaf!

ALBÓNDIGAS, DOS GENERACIONES

If you want to improve your health, one of the best things you can do is add more vegetables to your diet. This section has a lot of caldos (should I have written a whole section just for caldos?) because I believe caldos are a delicious way to incorporate more nutrient-dense foods into your everyday life, plus they are easy to make in one pot. On top of all that, caldos are always tasty meals!

I like to add zoodles to this caldo. My mom is the one who taught me to make albóndigas and when she saw me add zoodles, she thought it was so innovative. So, in that way, with this recipe, we learned from each other. Hence the name!

I don't want to burn my parents, but Monchi doesn't like tomatoes or onions at all. He loves albóndigas, though! So, guess what? My mom sneaks minced onion and tomato into each and every meatball she makes. Add that to the chayote, green beans, and zucchini that are already in the soup and you have a boastful serving of veggies at dinner time.

You can make the meatballs with ground turkey or ground beef. However you make it, the dish pairs amazingly well with tortillas de maiz and queso fresco. Plated that way, you have a satisfying meal! And as for the vegetables listed in the ingredients, they are just suggestions. Try your best to go with vegetables that you actually like. Dare to be creative and include your favorites here. After all, if you don't like it, then what is the point? s long as the vegetables you chose are not too starchy and are high in fiber, you are good!

PLATOS COMPLETOS

LONG
Over an hour.

DIFFICULTY
MEDIUM
YOU GOT THIS!!

SERVES
4

Ingredients:

For the meatballs
- 1lb of ground turkey breast or lean ground beef
- 1 tomato, chopped
- 1/2 of an onion, diced
- 1 or 2 garlic cloves, minced
- 1 tablespoon of pink Himalayan sea salt.
  (If you are using ground turkey, you can use Knorr chicken seasoning.)

For the soup
- About 1 cup of salsa roja
  (leftovers work great here)
- 1/2 of an onion, diced
- 1 clove of garlic, minced
- 1 zucchini, zoodled
- 1 carrot, diced
- 1 potato, diced
- 1 cup of green beans, ends cut off and cut into one-inch pieces (you can use frozen, pre-cut green beans to make your life easier. I sure do!)
- About 1 tablespoon olive oil
- 1 handful of cilantro, optional

Directions:

- Put your soup pot to warm over medium heat.
- After about a minute, add oil and allow it to warm for about another minute.
- Lower flame and sauté the diced onion and minced garlic until translucent and fragrant. Be careful to not burn it!
- Carefully pour in water until you fill the pot halfway and add the Knorr seasoning or salt. Cover and raise the heat to medium. Bring it all to a boil.
- As you wait for the broth to come to a boil, you can prepare the meatballs: in a bowl, mix ground meat, tomato, onion, garlic, and seasoning (with your hands) until they are well mixed together. Don't be shy! Really get your hands in there.
- Roll the meatballs into a sphere shape, about the size of ping pong balls. (One pound of ground meat makes about 16 meatballs.)
- Once your meatballs are formed and the broth is boiling, you can carefully plop them into the stew. Allow them to cook for about 45 minutes.
- While the meatballs are cooking, you can prepare your vegetables, washing and dicing as needed.
- After about 45 minutes, add the vegetables to the soup and cook for 15 more minutes.
- After the vegetables have cooked, stir in the salsa roja and optional cilantro. Allow it to boil with the soup for about 5 more minutes so that the flavors can infuse into the broth.

¡Buen provecho!

Señora Advice
*This goes great with corn tortillas and queso fresco.

CHICKEN TORTILLA SOUP, WITH LOVE FOR MONCHI

LONG
About an hour.

DIFFICULTY
EASY TO MEDIUM

SERVES 6

I am the youngest of five children. My siblings range from being ten to six years older than me. Due to this age gap, I was the last one of us to move out of my parents' house. My siblings were all married and had moved out while I was living at home, saving for my first home, and working on my career. Because of this, there was a time when it was just me and my mom and dad at home before I moved out. During these days, my mom would travel to El Salvador for a month at a time, leaving me and Monchi alone. And I would take the opportunity to experiment with cooking at home for my special audience of one. My dad was and still is a patient food tester.

Those days I made plenty of rookie mistakes, like cooking way too much food for just two people. Thankfully, my brother lived like five blocks away at the time and was always more than eager to come over and eat any extras.

This was a transitional time in which, being a young adult (barely past adolescence), I slowly started gaining confidence through trial and error at home. This soup es sabrosa, and it became one of Monchi's favorites. As a matter of fact, when I moved out into my own place and Monchi visited me, this was one of the first things I made for him. I hope you enjoy the recipe as much as we do.

Ingredients:

- 4 to 6 chicken legs (Remember that chicken leg bones make for a rich bone broth!)
- 1 can of tomato sauce
- 1 cup of leftover salsa roja
- 1 can of garbanzo beans
- 1 can of corn
- 1 can of kidney beans
- 1 can of black beans or pinto beans (leftovers work great here too)
- 1 carrot
- 1 onion
- 1 or 2 celery stalks
- 2 or 3 garlic cloves
- 1 tablespoon of pink Himalayan salt
- About 1 tablespoon of olive oil
- Toppings (as much as you would like)
  - Crushed tortilla chips
  - Avocado, diced
  - Shredded Mexican cheese blend

Directions:

- Wash the vegetables.
- Finely dice the carrot, onion, and celery into equally sized pieces.
- Mince the garlic cloves.
- Warm your large soup pot at medium heat, then add oil.
- Once the oil has heated for about a minute, add the carrot, onion, celery, and garlic. Stir. This will create your soup base.
- Once the veggies are fragrant, lower the flame. Be careful not to burn the vegetables. This is a gentle sauté!
- Once the onion is translucent, add filtered water and salt (or Knorr chicken seasoning) to your pot. This will become your broth. Bring this water to a boil at medium heat.
- In a second, separate pot, bring water to a boil and add the chicken legs for just about two minutes. This will remove any impurities from the bone.
- Throw out the water with the impurities and add the chicken legs to your soup base, which should be boiling by now.
- Cook the chicken legs in the soup base at medium heat for 15 minutes. Add apple cider vinegar at this time to help pull minerals from the bones and into your broth.
- While the chicken legs cook, open all the cans and rinse the contents well.
- After the chicken legs have cooked for about 15 minutes, add the tomato sauce, salsa roja, beans, and corn.
- Lower the flame, stir it all together, and bring to a simmer to combine flavors.
- Before serving, remove chicken legs to shred the meat. Dispose of the bones. This will allow for a more pleasant eating experience, without cumbersome bones.
- Once you serve the bowl of soup, top with crushed tortilla chips, diced avocado, and shredded cheese.

¡Buen provecho!

CALDO DE RES, BERNIE STYLE

LONG
Over an hour.

DIFFICULTY
MEDIUM
YOU GOT THIS!!

SERVES **6**

I know, I know. Sigo con los caldos. You already know I love caldos! (I promise there are different types of recipes coming!) The thing I love about caldos is that they are nutritious and comforting and you can feed a whole village with them if you strategize right. Caldo de res in particular warms me to the bone. The way I like to make it takes a little extra work, but it's totally worth it!

For extra nutrients, you can use meat with bones in it. This is going to make the broth extra gelatinous and fill it with amazing flavor. But first, you need to "purify" the bones. If you decide to make caldo with meat that doesn't have bones, you can skip this step.

Another useful tip: Once cooked, I like to cool the corn on the cob, cut the kernels off and put them into the broth. My Nana used to do that for me when she'd make me caldito de res. It saved me the trouble of trying to cut the corn over my bowl of soup! That little touch she added always showed she cared. When you make this caldo for yourself or for your loved ones, I hope you experience the loving feeling that is unique to a warm bowl of caldito.

Ingredients:

- 1lb of meat for caldo
- 1 onion
- 1 tomato
- 1 garlic clove
- 1 chile pepper
- 2 celery stalks
- 2 carrots
- 2 potatoes
- 1/2 of a cabbage
- 2 corn on the cob, cut in half
- 1 squash or chayote
- 1 yucca, optional
- 1 cup leftover salsa roja
- 1 tablespoon of olive oil
- Salt and pepper, al gusto

Directions:

- Bring some water to boil in a small pot and add the meat with the bones for a minute. Take it out of the water. This step is simply to remove any impurities from the bone. (You can skip this step if your meat is boneless.)
- Warm a larger pot over medium heat and add the olive oil. Put in the meat to sear until it's browned on all sides.
- Lower the heat to a simmer. Season the meat.
- Throw in the whole, peeled onion, the whole tomato, the garlic, the chile pepper and the celery stalk. Cover the pot. Let everything cook very slowly. You are looking for the moisture to escape the tomato, onion, and garlic. This, along with the meat, will create your soup base.
- Once the vegetables have become mushy and there's liquid, add water and stir so everything blends well together. Bring it all to a boil. Raise up the heat back to medium. Allow the meat to continue to cook.
- Once the meat is mostly cooked, you can remove the mushy vegetables. Those were to create a soup base, not to eat.
- While the soup comes to a boil, start chopping the rest of the vegetables: carrots, potatoes, cabbage, corn (keep it in the cob right now for extra flavor), squash or chayote, and the optional yucca.
- Once the meat has had some time to cook in the broth (about 30 to 45 minutes), add the vegetables to the boiling broth. Reduce the heat so that the soup is now at a simmer until the vegetables have cooked enough to soften. (About 15-20 minutes.)
- Throw some salsa roja into the broth and stir to really blend all the flavors together. Cook for 5-10 more minutes and enjoy!

¡Buen provecho!

Señora Advice
- Serve with lime and more salsa on the side.
- I especially love caldo de res with queso fresco and corn tortillas.
- Pink Himalayan salt and fresh cracked pepper are a great way to add more flavor.

PARTY TIME
BEEF POZOLE

In my family, we grew up eating red beef pozole. I've eaten chicken and pork pozole, sure, but my family isn't hugely into pork, so we never became accustomed to eating pork pozole. And, while my mom sometimes made chicken pozole and it was good, it just wasn't as thick and rich as beef pozole. There's something almost decadent about beef pozole with its gelatinous bone broth.

Beef pozole is another special comfort food that, in my family, is eaten on special occasions. For instance, a big batch can be made for a reunion or birthday party. When hosting parties, my family usually hires a taquero who makes tacos, rice, and beans, and, then, my mom makes a huge pot of pozole. This way, our guests have options.

Pozole is especially great for parties in cold months, like when my parents celebrate their winter birthdays. I have so many fond memories of parties in the garage or under tents, with the family gathering around pozole, and, later in the evening, warming up with some hot coffee.

Doña Rose says the key to a good pozole is a variety of cuts of beef. One year, she made pozole for el Willy's birthday party. She boasted that there were three cuts of beef in the pozole: chuck for its juicy meat, plus ribs, and neck for the bone broth. The bones make the broth extra rich. However, once cooked, I like to remove the meat from the pot, shred it, and then put it back in without the bone. That way, there are no cumbersome chunks or bones in anyone's bowl—just juicy and tender meat. (As you may have noticed in previous recipes, I do this with most caldos.) I think this extra step makes everyone's eating experience a little better.

Pozole has an amazing flavor on its own, but once I squeeze some lime on it, and add toppings such as finely cut cabbage and slices of rábanos, the dish is truly complete.

Ingredients:
- 1 lb of chuck beef
- 1 lb of rib meat
- 1 lb of carne con hueso
- 1 large can of maíz (hominy) for pozole or menudo
- 3 California chiles
- 2 roma tomatoes
- 1/2 of an onion
- 2 garlic cloves
- 2 serrano peppers
- 1 tablespoon of oregano
- Salt, al gusto
- Knorr beef seasoning, al gusto

Garnishes
- 1/2 of a cabbage, finely chopped
- 1 cup of radishes, sliced
- Lemons, al gusto

Directions:
To purify the bones, optional
- Bring some water to boil in a small pot and add the meat with the bones for a minute. Take it out of the water. This step is simply to remove any impurities from the bone.
(You can skip this step if your meat is boneless.)

Make the pozole
- Fill a pot halfway with water and add salt. Set to boil at high heat. Once boiling, put the meat to cook, heat to simmer. Cover and let cook for one hour.
- While the meat cooks, in a separate pot, put the tomatoes, chiles, garlic, and onion to boil with enough water to cover vegetables. Add a pinch of salt to the pot.
- Once boiled, strain the vegetables.
- Put boiled vegetables, a splash of water, and a pinch of salt in the blender until smooth to create a salsa base.
- Run this salsa base through a colander. Set it aside.
- Rinse the hominy. Add it, along with the salsa, Knorr beef-flavored seasoning, and oregano to the meat (soup) pot. Raise heat to medium high. Bring to a boil. (Break the oregano apart as you put it in the pot.)
- Once it boils, bring the heat down to a simmer for an hour to combine the flavors and cook evenly.
- Serve with sliced radishes, chopped cabbage, and lemon wedges.

¡Buen provecho!

LONG
Over an hour.

DIFFICULTY
EASY
You got this!

SERVES
10

MY JEFECITA'S AMAZING SOPES

My family is huge. I have two brothers and two sisters, and all of us are married. My parents say we went from being five kids to ten once our spouses joined the family. On top of that, my siblings and I have added seven of our own children to the family, so far. My mom boasts that her dynasty is nineteen and growing.

As you can imagine, I am no stranger to having a house full of people. (As I mentioned above, my immediate family currently consists of nineteen people.) And I learned from my mom and Nana that, as a matriarch, it is important to always be able to feed all your guests, especially family, when they come to visit.

As I talk about this, I recall a memory from when my husband and I had only been dating for about six months. I was still living with my parents, and el Willy dropped me off after hanging out. We were surprised to see that my siblings were all over to visit with their spouses and kids. It was a full house. As el Willy greeted everyone, my mom said to him, "Mijo, you're certainly staying for dinner, right?"

He shyly answered, "Well, you weren't expecting me, are you sure?"

To which my mom, with a sweet smile, kindly responded, "Of course I am. We were expecting you."

Without a single sign of despair, Mama Rose made sure to make enough food for her entire dynasty that day. In those early days of my relationship with el Willy, this was Mom's way of telling him bienvenido a mi dinastía or welcome to the family.

My mom didn't expect me to help since she knew I'd be busy keeping el Willy company and making him feel at home. So, he and I just hung out in the backyard with my nephews. The boys were so little back in those days! They jumped, raced, and did anything they could to impress their future tío. Later that afternoon, we ate sopes as a family. When I eat or make sopes now, I think back to that one special day in which el Willy started being part of my family.

MODERATE
Less than an hour.

DIFFICULTY
MEDIUM
difficulty to make
the sope base.
Easy to assemble.

SERVES
2

Ingredients:

- 1 cup of Maseca
- 1 medium russet potato
- Salt
- 1/2 lb of carne molida
- 1/4 of an onion
- 1 tomato
- 1 serrano pepper
- 1 cup Nana's Beans
- Chopped lettuce, enough to garnish your sopes
- Grated queso fresco, enough to garnish your sopes
- Salsa of your choice (pico, salsa roja, whatever you want)
- Cooking spray; I prefer avocado cooking spray

Directions:

Make the meat

- Put the pan on medium heat. Add a tiny bit of cooking spray and coat evenly.
- Put the ground beef to cook. Stir to avoid sticking and for even cooking.
- Add salt and pepper, al gusto.
- Add a chunk of onion (for flavor, we will remove it later).
- Add the tomato cut in fourths.
- Add the chile, with the stem cut off.
- Continue to stir for even cooking.
- Once the meat has evenly browned, lower heat to low. Cover the pan with the lid. Allow the meat to continue to cook on low for about 20 minutes.
- Once the meat is cooked, set it to the side for later.

Make the sopes

- While the meat cooks, peel a potato and cut it into fourths.
- Add the potato to a small pot of water with a teaspoon of salt. Set to medium heat.
- Allow the potato to boil. Once it boils, lower to a simmer. Cook until soft. Once cooked, remove potato and allow to cool.
- Add one cup of Maseca to a large bowl. Add a pinch of salt.
- Slowly add 1 1/2 cups of water and stir the mixture with your hands. You want the texture of play dough. You may not need all the water or you may need a little extra. Be patient and go little by little until you reach your desired consistency.
- Once the potato has cooled off a bit, mash it up.
- Add the mashed potato to the masa. Mix it in with your hands.
- Once thoroughly mixed, make a few balls of dough. You can make 4 large or 6 medium sized balls of dough.
- Wrap a ball in between plastic wrap and push it down with the bottom of a glass to create the desired dipped shape. Repeat with the rest of the dough until they all have that sope shape.
- Warm a pan to medium heat with enough oil to fry. You will cover the pan about an inch. Once the oil is hot, lower the flame to medium heat.
- Cook each sope using tongs and a spatula to evenly fry each side. You are looking for a beautiful golden color. Remove the sope and put on paper towels to absorb excess oil.
- Once all the sopes are fried, you are ready to assemble: use Nana's Beans as a base; then, add carne molida; next, top with lettuce, cheese, and salsa.
- Optional: add a drizzle of Mexican cream, if you wish!

¡Buen provecho!

MAMACITA'S RED ENCHILADAS

Right now, as I write this recipe, I am pregnant and on light bed rest. I am taking it easy as I adjust to a growing baby and a changing body. My mama has come over to help out and make me food so I do not have to trouble myself with cooking. (And because she wants to feed her youngest grandbaby who is gestating as I type, let's be real.)

For these reasons and for many others, I consider myself to be so blessed. When my mom was pregnant with me, she lived in the US and her mom was in El Salvador, so now she is giving me the motherly support (and food) she would have loved to have when she was pregnant.

I feel so grateful. Mama says she's doing it because she wants my baby boy to be gordito. After all, in our Mexican and Salvadorian cultures, we often call babies gorditos as a compliment. My dad says it's because it is rooted in a belief that a fat baby is well fed. And being well fed is a blessing. In my case, I was a skinny (scrawny, actually) kid; therefore, everyone always thought I was empachada, but that's a whole other story. So, as I was telling you, my mom is feeding me enchiladas as I rest because that's my antojo and she's happy to plump me up, and mother the heck out of me while I am in "my delicate condition."

I am about to become a mother and find myself being mothered more than ever before. It is a beautiful experience. It is nice to be self-aware enough at the moment to realize that I am creating a new memory. From now on, when I make or eat enchiladas, I will think fondly of my first pregnancy and my mom busting it down in my own kitchen.

MODERATE
About 45 minutes.

DIFFICULTY
MEDIUM
You got this!

SERVES **4**

Ingredients:
- 2 chicken breasts, cooked and shredded
- 3 guajillo chiles
- 3 California peppers
- 2 garlic cloves
- 1/2 of an onion
- Tortillas, enough to use up all the chicken (about 16)
- Grapeseed oil, a few tablespoons (for the different phases of cooking the enchiladas)
- Salt, al gusto
- Knorr chicken seasoning, al gusto
- Monterey Jack cheese, shredded; enough to fill your enchiladas and to optionally sprinkle it on top.

Directions:

- Bring water to a boil with salt to taste and a slice of onion.
- Once it boils, put the chicken breast to cook by poaching in water. Cook thoroughly without overcooking for about 15 minutes. Once cooked, remove the chicken and cool. When it's cool, shred it.
- While the chicken cooks and cools, rinse the chiles. Remove seeds and veins.
- Put the chile peppers in water and bring to a boil. After they have boiled for 5 minutes, turn off the flame. Let them rest in the hot water for 5 more minutes.
- In the blender, add 2 garlic cloves, about a teaspoon of salt, the cooked chiles, the rest of the onion, and a pinch of oregano. Add enough water to cover the ingredients.
- Blend until smooth.
- Warm a pan on medium heat with one tablespoon of oil.
- Add the liquefied sauce to the pan.
- Add about 1 teaspoon of Knorr chicken-flavored seasoning. Stir and allow it to bubble.
- Once it bubbles, turn off the flame. (We do not want to burn this sauce as this will make it bitter.) Set the salsa aside.
- In another bowl, set aside some Monterey Jack cheese.
- Warm a pan at medium heat, add enough grapeseed oil to cover the pan. Once the pan is warm, bring the heat down to low. With tongs, put a tortilla on the pan to warm briefly and cover with oil. (This is how my mama does it, and her enchiladas taste amazing! In an effort to avoid oil, I prefer to wrap the tortillas in a damp paper towel and microwave them for 30 seconds. Both methods work to make the tortillas more pliable and easy to work with. Try whichever option you prefer.)
- Next, dip the tortilla into the sauce. Cover both sides.

Assemble the enchilada

- Add shredded chicken and cheese on top of a prepared tortilla. Drizzle with a tiny bit of sauce. Fold your tortilla over.
- To pan fry the enchiladas, warm a comal and add a tiny drop of oil or cooking spray to prevent the saucy enchiladas from sticking to the comal.
- Warm your folded over and prepared enchilada evenly on both sides.
- Once warmed, set to the side and continue on until you are all done using the chicken and sauce!

¡Buen provecho!

Señora Advice
* Enjoy with lettuce, queso fresco, and sour cream on top! I personally love it with some radishes on the side as well.
* Instead of pan frying the enchiladas, like my mama does, you also have the option to assemble them all in a casserole dish, cover with cheese, and place them in the oven for 5-10 minutes at 350 degrees.

BERNIE'S SPICY GREEN ENCHILADAS

Now that you read about my mama's recipe for her delicious red enchiladas, I am ready to share my special recipe for green enchiladas with you!

El Willy and I have a vegetable garden in our backyard. We have zucchini, onion, radish, a variety of tomatoes, and more peppers than we know what to do with! One day, el Willy harvested so many chile peppers and tomatoes, it was almost overwhelming. There were Anaheim peppers, jalapeños, and serranos. Included in that day's harvest were tomatillos too. What a blessing! With all these beautiful green vegetables, I knew what I had to do—make green enchiladas, of course!

As I mentioned in the salsas section, my mom is popular among our friends and family for her red salsa and I'm popular for my green salsa. And it's the same with our enchiladas. My mom gets requests for her special red enchiladas, and I am praised for my green ones. My mom influenced my cooking style and taught me everything I know, yet each of us gravitate towards different ingredients. She is a master with dried California or guajillo peppers. Meanwhile, I find myself reaching for fresh green peppers, like Poblano, Anaheim, jalapeño, and serrano.

Whereas red enchiladas have a deep and robust flavor, green enchiladas are lighter and tangy. Which type of enchilada is your favorite? Are you team red or team green? I personally love both. It just depends on my mood.

PLATOS COMPLETOS

MODERATE
About 45 minutes.

DIFFICULTY
MEDIUM
You got this!

SERVES **4**

Ingredients:

- 2 chicken breasts
- 3 Anaheim chiles
- 1 jalapeño pepper, more if you prefer spicier food
- 1 serrano pepper, optional
- Lots of tomatillos. This is the main ingredient of the sauce! You want the tomatillos to make up about half of the sauce. Use your best judgment as they can vary in size.
- 2 garlic cloves
- 16 Tortillas
- Grapeseed oil
- Salt
- 1/2 of an onion
- 1 tablespoon salt
- 1 teaspoon Knorr chicken seasoning
- Monterey Jack cheese, shredded; enough to fill the enchiladas and cover them
- Olive oil, enough to coat the tortillas, optional
- One tablespoon of Maseca, optional

Directions:

- Bring water to a boil with salt to taste and a slice of onion.
- Once it boils, add the chicken breast to cook by poaching it in water. Cook thoroughly (without overcooking) for about 15 minutes. Once cooked, remove the chicken and cool. When it's cool, shred it. (You may also reserve some chicken broth.)
- While the chicken cooks and cools, rinse the chiles and tomatillos. Peel the garlic.
- Put the chiles, tomatillos, and garlic to roast in a comal. Once they have a beautiful and even toasted color, remove them from the comal.
- Carefully remove the seeds from the chiles. (Allow them to cool before doing so.)
- In a blender, add the roasted ingredients: 2 garlic cloves, tomatillos, and seedless chiles. Also add salt, 1/4 of the onion, and a handful of cilantro.
- Optional: add a splash of chicken broth at this point to get things going and for more flavor.
- Blend until smooth.
- Warm a saucepan on medium heat with one tablespoon of oil (or enough to evenly coat the pan) and a piece of onion to infuse the oil with extra flavor.

- Add the liquefied sauce to the pan and add 1 teaspoon of Knorr chicken-flavored seasoning to the sauce. Stir around in the pan, and allow it to bubble.
- Optional, if you want a thicker sauce, you can add one tablespoon of Maseca at this time and stir until dissolved.
- Once the sauce bubbles, turn off the flame. (We do not want to burn this sauce as it will turn bitter.)
- In another bowl, set aside some shredded Monterey Jack cheese.
- Warm another pan at medium heat, add enough grapeseed oil to cover the pan. Once the pan is warm, bring the heat down to low. With tongs, put a tortilla on the pan to warm briefly and cover with oil. (If you prefer to skip the oil, wrap the tortillas in a damp paper towel and microwave them for 30 seconds. Both methods work to make the tortillas more pliable and easy to work with. Try whichever option you prefer.)
- Next, dip the tortillas into the sauce. Cover both sides.

Assemble the enchilada

- Right in your casserole dish, add shredded chicken and cheese on top of a prepared tortilla. Drizzle the chicken and cheese with a tiny bit of sauce. (This tip is straight from my mama!)
- Fold your tortilla in thirds and turn it over with the seam down against the casserole dish.
- Continue to assemble the enchiladas in your casserole dish. Pack them tightly to maintain their shape.
- Once all your enchiladas are assembled, top with the remaining cheese and sauce. The saucier and cheesier, the better!
- Bake in the oven at 350 degrees for 5 to 10 minutes, so that the cheese melts but does not burn.
- Carefully remove the enchiladas and plate them!

¡Buen provecho!

Señora Advice
* You can top them with chopped onion, cilantro, Mexican crema, and lettuce!
* You can lightly season the shredded and cooked chicken with Knorr chicken flavored seasoning for even more flavor.

MY SUEGRITA'S PASTELITOS

My suegra makes some pretty delicious pastelitos. During the first trimester of my pregnancy, I was craving these delicious treats but, between working a full-time job and writing this book, I was too exhausted to make my suegrita's pastelitos. Somehow she must have known because, one day, she showed up to my casa with pastelitos in hand. Our theory is that her grandbaby telepathically asked her for the antojo. It would not be the first time during the pregnancy that I got pampered by my suegra's intuition and instinct.

My suegra is deeply in touch with her indigenous roots and ancestral knowledge. And I am humbled and honored that she shares the wisdom passed down from her mother and grandmother with me. It is like being welcomed into her dynasty.

Her traditional knowledge came out in full force when I was pregnant. She advised me to wear red clothing in order to protect my energy and the baby's, and to stay home during eclipses, with the shutters closed. As I got closer to my due date, she told me all about the phases of the moon and their relationship to pregnancy, and how a full moon is thought to help in el parto or delivery. Through all this, I felt closer to her than ever. What a beautiful feeling to be so mothered as I am about to become a mother myself. Te digo, I wish everyone had a suegra like her! Her wisdom runs deep, she has so much love to give, and her pastelitos are mouth-watering.

Try these pastelitos today and share some with your pregnant or too-busy-to-cook friends. These pastelitos are relationship-building; I am telling you! The pastelito dough is made of Maseca and the filling usually contains cooked meat and a ton of minced vegetables. Season the dough and stuff it well for a flavorful meal.

PLATOS COMPLETOS

LONG
About an hour.

DIFFICULTY
MEDIUM
to *señora* level

SERVES
6

Ingredients:

- 1/2 lb of ground beef
- 1/4 of an onion, diced
- 2 or 3 garlic cloves, minced
- 1 carrot
- 1 bell pepper
- 1 russet potato
- 1 cup of chopped green beans
- Instant corn flour (I use Maseca, you can choose your favorite). To make the masa, mix 2 cups of instant corn flour with 2 cups of water. (The measurement here is hard, so this is what I do: if I make too much masa, I use the leftover to make tortillas; if I don't make enough, then I mix a little more Maseca and water.)
- 2 tablespoons of paprika
- 1 tsp of grapeseed oil to sauté plus a lot more for later to fry the pastelitos

Directions:

- Wash and dry the produce. Peel the carrots and potatoes.
- Warm a nonstick pan on medium heat. Add a little bit of oil, enough to evenly and thinly cover the pan. Less is more!
- Add the ground beef on medium heat. Season with salt and pepper. Move it around and break it up to brown it evenly.
- Once browned, lower the flame to the lowest setting and cover the ground beef with a lid.
- While the ground beef cooks slowly, chop up the carrots, potatoes, green beans, and bell peppers. I suggest using a food processor to make this easier on your hands. It saves time too!
- Add the chopped carrots, potatoes, green beans, and bell peppers. Raise the heat to medium. Stir all the ingredients around to ensure even cooking.
- After about 15 minutes, the ground beef mixture is cooked and you can turn off the flame.

- While the meat and veggies cool off slightly, start preparing your masa. Mix together masa and water until you have the desired consistency (like play dough). Add paprika to the masa for a splash of color.
- Heat some grapeseed oil in a frying pan at medium to low heat.
- By now, the ground beef and veggies will be cooled down.
- In the palm of your hand, gather a ball of dough and begin to flatten it.
- Add meat to the center of your masa and now fold the masa over to trap the meat in, like a dumpling or empanada.
- Pinch the edges to ensure no meat comes out. (Be very gentle during this process. You don't want to crush them too hard or the meat will come out.) Pat the meat inside the masa, to ensure even distribution. If any spots look thin, you can always patch them up with a tiny amount of masa.
- As you assemble the pastelitos, place them carefully in the oil to fry them.
- A spatula is best to use here, as tongs may be too rough for the delicate pastelitos.
- As you fry the pastelitos, they will turn a beautiful golden color. Be sure not to burn them, and cook them on each side for even cooking.
- Put them in a bowl with several paper towels to drain out any excess oil.

¡Buen provecho!

Señora Advice
*Enjoy them with salad and salsa as a meal, or on their own as a snack!

LA MERA MERA'S ARROZ A LA VALENCIANA (PAELLA)

In El Salvador, paella is called arroz a la valenciana. It has this name due to the Spaniard influence. Paella is a lot like risotto. I included it in this section because it is a complete meal on its own. I love the practicality of making it in one pot that can feed a family or a large group of friends. For this reason, I love making it for dinner parties, paired with some Spanish wine. It is absolutely divine. Whenever I make it for guests, they typically request seconds because it is so delicious!

Paella usually has seafood and, as I mentioned in some recipes ago, my mom is terribly allergic to seafood. Therefore, she specially created this recipe with chicken, ham, and beef sausage, and taught it to me.

I'm going to keep it 100% real with you all. This is a cookbook, yes, but it is also so much more than that. I want this book to take the intimidation out of cooking, and I also want this book to be honest about how to make cooking fit into your life. And I have to tell you a secret—rice is my kryptonite. Sopita de arroz, arroz con leche, rice with vegetables: you name it, I love it. However, rice dishes always take me longer to learn and I'm not sure why. Paella, as you can imagine, was no exception.

The first time I made this meal, it was with my mom. It came out great because I made it under her expert supervision. I considered myself a chingona and set off to make it for myself and by myself the following week only to end up with a soggy mess. I added too much water and prematurely stirred

and over-stirred. The next time my mom and I made this dish together, I took more diligent notes.

My point? If at first you don't succeed, try again! Try until you nail it. If I had never tried to make paella again after that first epic fail of mine, then I would have never mastered a dish that impresses so many of my friends when they come over. Read on and see if you can get this right the first or second time, or, if you're like me, the third time.

LONG
Over an hour.
Patience is key!

DIFFICULTY
Get ready to bust out
señora skills

SERVES **6**

Ingredients:
- 2 cups of white rice
- 3 cups of warm water
- 2 all-beef franks, cut in slices
- 3 chicken thighs
- 1 ham steak, cut in cubes
- 1 red bell pepper
- 1 small onion
- 1 garlic clove
- 1 celery stalk
- 3 roma tomatoes
- 1 envelope of saffron seasoning
- 1 pinch paprika
- 1 (tiny) pinch of oregano
- 1 pinch dried parsley
- Adobo seasoning, to taste
- 1 cup of mixed vegetables: peas, corn, and carrots (frozen or canned works here)
- Grapeseed oil (or your preferred vegetable oil for sautéing), enough to thinly and evenly coat your pans
- 1 tablespoon of Knorr chicken seasoning

Directions:

- Pan fry the chicken with oil and some adobo seasoning. You will know it's cooked when it has an even, beautiful golden color. It may even look caramelized. Once cooked, set aside. We will be putting the cooked chicken into the paella later.
- Chop the ham steak into cubes and the all-beef franks into slices (like when you make huevos con weenies). Sauté them in separate pans with a little oil until they are fragrant and have an even color.
- Set aside the three different cooked meats in separate bowls. We will come back to them.
- Finely chop the onion, celery, tomato, bell pepper, and mince the garlic.
- Put your paella pan to warm at medium heat, ensure it's evenly covered with a thin layer of oil.
- Sauté the chopped vegetables for one minute.
- Next, add rice and one tablespoon of Knorr chicken seasoning along with paprika, dried parsley, and a tiny pinch of oregano.

- When the rice looks crispy and it's sticking together, add the chicken, sausage, and ham. Continue to stir to blend the flavors.
- Add one cup of water and the peas, carrots, and corn. (The water keeps the ingredients from sticking together.)
- In two cups of water, dissolve the saffron seasoning. Stir.
- Add the water and saffron mixture to the pan. Gently stir to combine flavors and ingredients. Lower heat to simmer and cover.
- Check on it periodically, but ensure not to over-stir past this point! (Over-stirring has messed it up for me in the past!)
- When the water has evaporated (in about 20 minutes), the dish is done!
- Once cooked, fluff up the rice in the pan before serving.

¡Buen provecho!

Señora Advice
*If your rice happens to stick to the edges in the cooking process, you can always add a splash of water.

LA JEFA'S CHILES RELLENOS

Now that you know that seafood was taboo in my house, you can imagine that my mama had to get creative for meatless Fridays during Lent. Let me tell you, she came up with a lot of good stuff, and I looked forward to her Lent dishes, such as tacos de papa or enchiladas de queso. But my absolute favorite Lent recipe was, and still is, her chiles rellenos! I am almost drooling now as I think of them.

When I was first dating my husband years ago, I asked my mama to teach me to make chiles rellenos. She punked me the whole time! Let's be honest, no one can burn you better than your own mama, and mine is no exception: "Wow, you get a boyfriend and all of a sudden you're interested in making chiles rellenos. I see how it is."

I won't lie, the process intimidated me at first. (My jefa's teasing probably didn't help.) Without the right tools, and without patience, it's quite easy to fail miserably. Pero don't even trip, I will walk you through the process, step by step. Together, we can figure out this recipe that I used to think was only for super experienced señoras.

LONG
Over an hour.

DIFFICULTY
SEÑORA LEVEL.
Make your mama proud!

SERVES
2

Ingredients:

- 4 green pasilla peppers
- 1/4 block of Monterey Jack cheese
- 3 eggs (separated: 3 egg whites, 2 egg yolks)
- 3 tablespoons of all purpose flour
- Grapeseed oil, enough to evenly coat the pan to fry the chiles
- Salsa roja for garnish

Directions:

- Rinse the chiles. Pat dry.
- On a comal, char the chiles evenly on each side.
- Put the charred chiles in a plastic bag, close the bag, and let the chiles sit for 15 minutes. After that, peel each chile with your hands. The peel should slide right off after resting in the plastic bag.
- Slice each chile down the middle, while keeping the tip and stem of the chile intact. Clean/cut out seeds.
- Add a slice of cheese that's appropriate to the size of the chile. You can also stuff with shredded cheese. (If you have leftover cheese at the end of this, save it for quesadillas!)
- After each chile has been stuffed with cheese, set aside.
- Separate the egg yolks from the egg whites. With a hand mixer, beat the egg whites until fluffy and foamy. Beat in the egg yolks to give the egg mixture a more vibrant color.
- Set a plate with flour.
- Set your frying pan to medium heat. Once warm, coat evenly with grape seed oil.
- While that warms up, lightly and evenly coat a chile with flour.
- Then dip the chile in the egg mixture. To keep the integrity of the cut and stuffed chile, be gentle. Only dip one side. Put the chile in the warmed pan, with the dipped part into the mixture touching the oil. Once you place the chile in the pan, apply a spoonful of egg mixture on top. This is how you evenly and carefully coat the chile. Cook evenly on both sides.
- You will know it's ready to flip when the egg mixture begins to change in texture and get a beautiful golden color.
- Set each chile aside once it's cooked.
- Serve drizzled with salsa roja.

¡Buen provecho!

Señora Advice

* To avoid sticking to the pan, you can spoon oil from the same pan over the edges of the chile as it cooks.

* Cook one chile at a time so you can really give it the TLC it needs and deserves.

CLASSIC PUPUSAS

MODERATE
Less than an hour.

DIFFICULTY
MEDIUM TO SEÑORA LEVEL

SERVES 4

I may be half Salvadorian-American, but I 100% love pupusas, that chubby tortilla stuffed with cheese and beany goodness, hand patted to perfection. When I have to explain pupusas to people who don't know what the heck they are, I simply describe the gooey stuff trapped inside the cooked masa. I've also told friends they are basically flat stuffed dumplings.

When I was tiny, I loved watching my mom make pupusas. She would even give me a piece of masa to play with, so I could practice patting. Normally, though, I'd just end up making a doll or some special shape out of the masa. That, or I'd enjoy balling it up and then smooshing it between my hands over and over again. ¡Desmadrosa!

My favorite thing to do with the masa, however, was to make my mom a tiny tortilla out of it. When my mom and I make pupusas together now that I am an adult, I always make her a tiny tortilla as a joke, for old-time sake. I always say my family's pupusas are better than anything you can get at a restaurant, but I might be biased.

I promise you, homemade pupusas are incredibly satisfying. So, if you have a free day to throw down in the kitchen Salvi style, I recommend you try this recipe out.

This recipe is actually two in one. Pupusas and curtido go together like peanut butter and jelly, so they shall remain together in this cookbook too. First, you prepare the masa for the pupusas along with the filling. You can fill the pupusas with cheese or cold beans mixed with cheese. If you have leftover cold, mashed beans on hand, that's perfect. Pupusas are a great way to use leftover beans. Next, you need to make curtido, which is also a bit of work. So, feel free to make the curtido ahead of time. It'll be good in the fridge for up to five days, although I often keep it for longer. (Fermentation equals probiotics which equals gut health!)

Ingredients:

- 1 pinch of salt
- 3 cups of instant corn flour (I use Maseca)
- 3 cups of water
- 2 cups of cold leftover mashed beans (Nana's Beans work great for this)
- 1/2 cup of grated cotija cheese
- 1/2 cup of grated Monterey cheese

Directions:

- Mix the beans and cheese together.
- Mash the beans and cheese together in a bowl to create a paste. This paste-like texture is what you want inside of the pupusas. If the beans are too runny, they may leak out of the pupusas.
- Mix the Maseca and salt together in a bowl with your hands. Gradually add water to create masa. Start with Maseca first and slowly, little by little, add water. Proceed to mix in the water with your hands. Continue to gradually add water and mix until you have the consistency of play-dough. When the masa doesn't stick to your hands anymore, it's ready. You may need to use all the water or you may need an extra splash of water to get the right texture.
- Before you begin to assemble the pupusas, warm up your comal on medium to low heat.
- Roll up about 12 evenly sized balls of masa. Cover with a damp towel to avoid drying out. (I like to do it this way, but my mom and suegra make them as they go. Use whichever method you prefer!)
- Put one ball of masa in your hand. With the other hand, mold the masa to create a bowl or reservoir.
- Add the bean and cheese mixture to the middle of your "masa bowl." Enough to fill that reservoir in the masa.

- Work the outside masa around the beans to cover them. You want to trap them inside the masa.
- Now, begin to palmear. Use your palms to flatten out the pupusa. The goal here is to pat the pupusa flat and to work the beans and cheese all the way to the edges.

  This patting technique requires a lot of practice, so don't get discouraged if you don't get it right away!
- Add the pupusa to the comal, cooking each side for about 4 minutes. It should become fragrant, like the aroma of a cooked tortilla. You want each side to get a beautiful golden color. Avoid burning.

¡Buen provecho!

Señora Advice

*You can moisten your hands between assembling each pupusa to avoid the masa sticking to your hands or drying on your hands. My mom moistens her hands with water. My suegra moistens her hands with oil. Try both and see what works best for you!

*If some beans seep out from the middle, you can always add a little bit of masa to patch it up.

*Enjoy with curtido and salsa roja!

CURTIDO FOR PUPUSAS

FAST
Less than 30 minutes.

DIFFICULTY
MEDIUM

SERVES
12
About a dozen. It all depends on how much you use to top your pupusa.

When I was little, I would eat my pupusas on their own. Like if my pupusa was a slice of pizza or something. As I got older, I came to enjoy the way curtido compliments the pupusa. Now, as an adult, I believe a pupusa is not complete without curtido and salsa roja.

Curtido is a lightly pickled dish that, if you ask me, is a Salvi superfood. Similar to sauerkraut, the main ingredient in curtido is cabbage. Yet, curtido is only lightly fermented, and, therefore, has a much milder taste than sauerkraut! Due to the light fermentation and pickling, curtido offers the benefits of being a vegetable dish and a source of probiotics.

During my fifth month of pregnancy, I took a nutrition class to learn all about the best foods to eat to nourish my body and my gestating baby boy. Some tips I learned were to eat probiotics, brightly colored fruits and vegetables, lots of protein, foods high in calcium, lots of iron, you get the idea.

After the class, the nutritionist and I had a private consultation over the phone. I shared with her that, during my pregnancy, I craved the comfort foods of my culture: curtido being one of them. She validated that nutritious food knows no culture. Nutritious food can be found in our traditional meals. The beans in the pupusas offer iron. The cheese inside the pupusas offers calcium. Y curtido? Pues, I could hear her excitement over the phone when I told her about curtido. It seemed like a nutritionist's dream come true! Probiotics and vegetables. She was eager to try it for herself and encouraged me to continue to eat it.

So, enjoy this curtido along with your pupusas or however else you would like. My husband loves it on top of hotdogs, for example. I love it on top of plain salads for an extra kick. What's your favorite way to enjoy curtido? However you enjoy it, be excited that you are nourishing your body with a Salvi superfood that offers you probiotics and a serving of vegetables. If you ask me, it's all about being good to our bodies and taste buds at the same time!

Ingredients:

- 1/2 cup of apple cider vinegar
- 1 teaspoon of oregano
- 1/2 of a cabbage, finely cut
- 1 carrot, grated
- 1 chile pepper, sliced (a pepperoncini works great here! You can also use a jalapeño), optional
- 1/2 of a red onion, sliced
- Salt, al gusto (I love pink Himalayan salt for more nutrients)
- Boiled water, enough to cover the vegetables

Directions:

- Bring water to boil as you rinse and chop all of the vegetables.
- Place the rinsed, chopped vegetables in a large, heat-safe bowl.
- Pour boiling water over vegetables, just enough to cover vegetables. Allow to cool.
- Once cool, discard any liquid. It is OK if the vegetables remain a bit wet.
- Add vinegar, salt, and oregano. Stir to combine flavors.
- Store in a glass container with an airtight lid.
- Cover and refrigerate. The longer it marinates, the more flavor it will have!

¡Buen provecho!

Señora Advice
*The curtido can be stored in the fridge for about a week.

TACOS DORADOS SONORA STYLE WITH SOPA DE FIDEOS

Tacos dorados was one of the first dishes I learned to cook. See, I was only fourteen years old when my oldest sister got married. (She is nine years older than I am.) In my sister's newlywed days, my mom taught her to make these tacos and, of course, I was in the middle of both of them, metichando como siempre. Hey, this was (and still is) one of my favorite foods of all time, and I wanted to learn how to make it too! Since I've been making these tacos for more than half of my life, I am now more than comfortable and confident making them.

When el Willy and I were first dating, my suegra was, unfortunately, dealing with some health issues. (Gracias a Dios, she is better now.) Her ill health was affecting her appetite and she was not eating much. One day, I decided to go over and make this meal for her. Sure, I was nervous. I was cooking for my future suegra! But I knew I could not fail with these trusty tacos. (As I am writing this, my mouth is watering for tacos fritos filled with slow cooked tri-tip meat and sopa de fideos made with the consomé of the meat.) That day, el Willy's whole family joined us for the meal and they seemed to like it. My suegra ate more than we had seen her eat in a while. Whew! I was relieved. He later told me that in the days that followed, my suegrita called her sisters to boast about her oldest son's girlfriend: "Fíjate que la muchacha llegó y me cocinó una comida muy rica. Sí, es muy buena para cocinar. ¡Bendito sea Dios!"

El Willy is the oldest, he's a boy, and he holds a special place in my suegra's heart (that's code for he's the favorite). If this meal impressed her, I promise you will love it too!

This recipe also includes directions on how to make sopa de fideos. The slow-cooked meat in the tacos will give you a broth base that is great for making a sopita that serves as a delicious appetizer for these tacos dorados!

LONG
2 hours to cook the meat. Plus about 30-45 minutes to make the tacos.

DIFFICULTY
MEDIUM

SERVES 4

Ingredients:

For the tacos
- 1/2 lb of tri-tip meat
- 1 onion
- 1 or 2 garlic cloves
- Tortillas, enough for all the meat
- Grapeseed oil, enough to fry the tacos
- Salt, al gusto
- Garnishes of your choice: pico de gallo, lettuce, sour cream, you get the idea

For the sopa de fideos
- 1 cup pasta of your choice (fideos, coditos, or shells)
- 1 small can of tomato sauce, or one cup of salsa roja
- 1 handful of fresh cilantro
- Garnishes of your choice: lemon, lime, Tajín, or Tapatío, al gusto

Directions:

- Put the tri-tip in a soup pot with salted water and add a whole (peeled) onion and 1 or 2 cloves of garlic. You will simmer this on low for two hours.
- Once the tri-tip is cooked, remove it from the water along with the onion and the garlic. Save the broth! This makes a great base for sopa de fideos. Allow the tri-tip to cool.
- You can make the sopa while you wait for the meat to cool.

Sopa de fideos

- Break some raw noodles into one or two-inch pieces. (Skip this step if you are using coditos or shells instead of noodles.) Toast the pasta on a comal until they catch a golden color.
- Bring the broth back to a boil and add canned tomato sauce or salsa roja.
- Once boiling, add the toasted noodles and a handful of cilantro. Cook for 10 minutes or according to the pasta's directions.

Tacos Dorados

- Shred the cooled meat.
- Put your frying pan on the stove to warm up on medium heat. Once warm (after about a minute), add grapeseed oil. You want enough oil to cover the pan, about an inch.
- Put the meat into the corn tortilla and fold.
- Using tongs, hold the shape of the taco together and submerge the fold into the oil, holding it for a few seconds. After that, gently release the taco from the tongs and lay it on its side.
- Keep adding tacos in this way until the pan is full. Use the same tongs or a spatula to flip them.
- Make sure to cook the tacos evenly on both sides.
- Once crispy and golden, remove the tacos from the pan and stand upright in a bowl lined with paper towels to absorb any excess oil from the tacos.

¡Buen provecho!

Señora Advice

*You can garnish tacos with your favorite toppings: shredded lettuce, pico de gallo, guac, and queso fresco are all great options!
*Enjoy the sopita with a squeeze of lime and a pinch of Tajin or Tapatio!
*The curtido can be stored in the fridge for about a week.

NO-FRY TAQUITOS

Tacos dorados are one of my favorite foods but I do not eat them very often since they are fried in oil. I sometimes make them when I am hosting friends and want to show off, or I'll enjoy a taco dorado on my own here and there as a mindful indulgence.

Most of the time, however, I'll opt for taquitos, aka flautas, instead. I bake them in the oven until they are crispy. Making them in the oven means, of course, less oil, and less oil means it's a bit healthier, which is great. It allows me to have an authentic taste while making the option slightly better for my health. Another great thing about these taquitos is that you can use leftover chicken breast or a rotisserie chicken to make them. That way, you can skip the slow cooking of the meat (from the previous recipe) if you are short of time.

Taquitos also carry a special charm because they are dipping foods. This makes them great for potlucks, like when your homies come over to watch a boxing match or football game. I personally love to dip taquitos into guac or sour cream. On the side, I'll have some rábanos dressed in lime and Tajín and some homemade pickled onions. You can also chop up some romaine lettuce and sprinkle a little bit of queso fresco on top to serve on the side. I'll have all these little dipping sauces and side dishes in their own matching bowls for major presentation points.

Done this way, you have a fun and even interactive meal that feels like a tapa. Es tan sabroso que no one will even notice they were baked instead of fried!

Ingredients:
- 16 tortillas
- 2 chicken breasts, cooked and shredded
- Cooking spray (I like avocado oil spray)
- Salsa of your choice (salsa roja, salsa verde, or mixed salsa), for adding flavor to the cooked chicken.
- 1 teaspoon of Knorr chicken-flavored seasoning
- Salt, al gusto

Directions:
Cook the chicken
- Poach chicken breast in salted, boiling water for 15 minutes at medium low heat.
- After the chicken has finished cooking, set it on a plate to cool.
- Preheat your oven to 400 degrees.
- Shred the chicken with two forks.
- Mix the shredded chicken with about 2 tablespoons of salsa, just enough to coat the chicken and give it some color.
- Evenly season the cooked, shredded chicken with Knorr chicken flavored seasoning, al gusto.

If you are using seasoned, leftover chicken, skip the above steps
- Spray your baking sheet or casserole dish with cooking spray.
- Cover a stack of tortillas (8 at a time) with damp paper towels. Microwave for 30 seconds. This will make the tortillas pliable and easy to work with.
- Place the cooked, seasoned chicken in your prepared tortilla and roll it, like a flauta.
- As you roll each taquito, place it onto a baking sheet or casserole dish. (I like to place them with the fold down, so they retain their form.)
- As you roll each taquito, mist it with cooking spray.
- Place the taquitos in the casserole dish close to each other. If they are closer to each other, they will hold up their form better. (Don't forget to continue to mist each taquito with cooking spray! This will help the taquitos crisp up in the oven.)
- Put the taquitos in the oven at 400 degrees for 20 to 25 minutes. (Watch them closely for the last 5 minutes to make sure they get a beautiful, even, golden color, but do not burn.)

¡Buen provecho!

MODERATE
About 45 minutes.

DIFFICULTY
MEDIUM

SERVES
4

HERENCIA TACOS

In the drinks section, I mentioned that el Willy and I created a cocktail together to embody what it means to me to be SalviMex in Los Angeles. I am happy to say that I am including a recipe with a similar concept in this section as well. This is a dish that was exclusively created for this book, that is uniquely SalviMex.

I went to la Mera Mera with the idea for creating a Los Angeles-based SalviMex fusion recipe. Who better to ask help from? After all, she molded me into the woman and home cook that I am. I wish I could say we brainstormed this together, but this idea is all hers! It came to her as soon as I was finished explaining myself, as if we were on the same frequency.

So, what did my jefecita do? She made this recipe for me on my birthday! There we were—my husband, my parents, and I—celebrating my thirtieth birthday together with delicious food. We were testing the recipe for this book, but it didn't feel like work at all. In fact, Monchi normally likes his tacos plain, but he was a good sport and tried this recipe complete with the garnishes and sides. Let me tell you—it was so good, that even Monchi was singing its praises!

So, what exactly does this recipe consist of?

It is a taco, much like the tacos dorados from my father's arsenal of family recipes, influenced by his home state of Sonora. Inside the taco, you will find shredded beef that has been sofrito lightly with a tasty salsita. (My mom and I love our salsas, remember?) To top off the taco, instead of the usual guac or pico de gallo, there's a unique curtido. Instead of normal vinegar, this curtido was pickled with the vinegar from a jalapeño jar! In this curtido, you will find jalapeños, cabbage, carrots, and onion. For an extra kick, you will also notice that we added Tajín! (Remember, I really love Tajín.)

This recipe really has something for everyone, especially for those who love flavorful food!

Enjoy this meal with chopped cucumbers or sliced rábanos on the side and an Herencia Cocktail to drink. I hope you will love this meal as much as I do. When I eat it, I will think of everyone who read this book and made the recipe for themselves. When you eat it, I hope you feel like you are a guest at my home.

¡Buen provecho!

LONG
Over 2 hours,
but so worth it!

DIFFICULTY
DIFFICULT
Señora level

SERVES
6

Ingredients:

- 11 lb of tri-tip
- Tortillas, enough for the meat
- 2 roma tomatoes
- 1 guajillo pepper
- 1 California pepper
- 1 garlic clove
- Salt, al gusto
- 1 teaspoon Mrs. Dash seasoning
- 1 teaspoon Knorr beef flavored seasoning
- 1 tablespoon olive oil, to sofreir the salsa
- Grapeseed oil, enough to evenly coat your frying pan to fry the tacos

For the curtido
- 1/2 of a cabbage
- 2 carrots
- 1 red onion
- 1 can pickled jalapeños
- 1 pinch of oregano
- Tajín, al gusto

Directions:

- Slow cook the tri-tip in salted water at medium to low heat.

While the meat cooks, make the curtido!

- Wash and cut the cabbage, carrot, and red onion.
- Mix the chopped ingredients in a large heat-proof bowl. Season with oregano.
- Pour boiling water over the mix, just enough to cover the vegetables. Let it rest for half an hour, until the water cools. Once cool, strain out the water.
- Add the jar of pickled jalapeños, vinegar and all. Mix well.
- Season with Tajín and enjoy.

Back to the meat

- Once cooked, allow it to cool.
- Once the meat is cool enough to handle, shred it.

As the meat cools, make your sauce!

- Clean the chiles (remove seeds, veins and stems) and boil them along with the tomato and garlic.
- Strain the water from the ingredients.
- In a blender, put the chiles, garlic, tomato, and salt. Blend until you have a smooth consistency.
- On medium heat, warm a pan. Add olive oil.
- Add the sauce and a teaspoon of Mrs. Dash and a teaspoon of beef-flavored Knorr seasoning.
- Once the sauce bubbles, fold in the shredded meat.
- Stir until the meat is evenly coated. You want a thick consistency here. (Not runny.)
- Turn off the heat, and cover the pan.

Fry the tacos

- Set a frying pan to medium heat.
- Cover with about an inch of grapeseed oil.
- Once the oil is warm, prepare the tortilla by adding the shredded meat inside.
- With tongs, place the taco to fry. Using the tongs, hold the shape of the taco together from the opening, so that it is upright, and fold-side down in the oil. Hold it for a few seconds. This will help to give the taco its shape.
- After a few seconds, gently release it into the oil. Ensure to cook the tacos evenly on both sides.
- Keep adding tacos in this way until the pan is full. Use the same tongs or a spatula to flip them.
- Once crispy and evenly golden, remove the tacos from the pan and stand upright in a bowl lined with paper towels to absorb any excess oil from the tacos.

Enjoy the tacos with curtido inside of them!

Señora Advice
* Note: You can store the curtido in a glass jar!

PANES CON POLLO

We are reaching the end of this book. When we reach the end of the year, there are certain foods my family eats. If we don't eat that special food, it feels as if the holiday season hasn't started, so I'd like to end this book with the same foods that I end every year with. First off, panes con pollo. My side of the family eats this every holiday season! Usually, we eat it on New Year's Eve. El Willy's side of the family eats this on Christmas Eve.

The dish consists of chicken cooked in a delicious sauce, put into a pan francés or bolillo, and then garnished with cucumber, tomato, and watercress. It is mouth-watering, delicious, and comforting.

As I said in the beginning of the book, my dad is Mexican-American and my mom is Salvadorian-American. Because of this SalviMex upbringing in our bilingual home, a mix of Salvi caliche, Mexican modismos (specifically from Sonora), and South East Los Angeles slang peppered our daily conversations. Sometimes we used terms interchangeably. For instance, on some occasions, I may say puchica. Other times I may say chale. In addition, I consider myself to be a chingona, cachimbona and badass mujer all at once.

I am sharing this with you all for context. Yes, my family knew this dish was called panes con pollo (or sometimes pavo). But, remember how I described this dish? Chicken with sauce in a bolillo or pan francés. A lot of Mexicans refer to chicken in sauce as mole. And, a lot of Mexicans refer to sandwiches with bolillo bread as tortas. So, at home, sometimes we referred to panes con pollo as tortas de mole salvadoreño. Yeah, imagine me eating panes con pollo around my in-laws and calling it that. I'm sure in the beginning they were asking el Willy, "Are you sure this girl is really half Salvi?"

Whatever the heck you call it, this meal is a huge part of my life. It's juicy, flavorful, and carries the familiar nostalgia that only a holiday recipe can offer.

I have outlined how to make a small amount of this recipe. For special occasions, you can certainly make more! Simply increase the ingredients.

LONG
Over an hour.

DIFFICULTY
MEDIUM TO DIFFICULT

SERVES 4

Ingredients:

- 2 chicken breasts
- 2 to 3 tomatoes, to make the sauce
- 1/2 of an onion
- 1 teaspoon of lemon pepper
- 1 teaspoon of oregano
- 1 to 2 garlic cloves
- 1 tablespoon of worcestershire sauce
- 1 tablespoon of mustard
- 1 tablespoon of vinegar
- 1/2 of a carrot
- 1/2 of a potato
- Salt, al gusto
- Olive oil, for pan frying the chicken
- 4 bolillos or panes franceses
- 1 tomato, sliced
- 1/2 of a cucumber, sliced
- Watercress or spinach, about a handful
- Mayo, enough to spread evenly across the bread, optional

Directions:

- Wash and chop the vegetables (minus the garnishes). The tomato can be cut into fourths. The carrot and potato should be peeled and sliced. Set them to the side.
- Rinse the chicken breast with water and place it in a bowl with cool water and a splash of vinegar for a few minutes.
- Remove the chicken breast and rub with about a tablespoon of mustard.
- Heat a pan on medium heat. Once warm, add enough olive oil to evenly, yet thinly, coat the pan.
- Add the chicken breast. Season with salt, lemon pepper, and oregano. Cook for about 5-7 minutes on each side.
- As it cooks, add tomato, onion, garlic, and a splash of water to a blender. Blend until smooth.
- Run through a colander and pour on top of your evenly cooked chicken.
- Add a splash of worcestershire sauce to the saucy, cooked chicken and stir.
- At this time, add the carrot and potatoes.
- Lower the heat to medium and cover the pan.
- Allow this to cook until the chicken can be easily shredded.
- Once the chicken is cooked, you can rinse and slice your garnishes.

Assemble the sandwich

- Cut a bolillo or pan francés lengthwise, stuff with the saucy chicken, and garnish with tomato, cucumber, and watercress.

¡Buen provecho!

SALVADORIAN TAMALES

I remember when I visited El Salvador at the age of seventeen: I had a pixie cut and had died my bangs a blue green color. My cousins were fascinated by their "American cousin" and jokingly called me their prima, la gringa. Meanwhile, I was enthralled because I had never seen so much greenery in my life. I was also excited to bond with so many cousins.

My abuelita, tías, and older primas welcomed my mom, my dad, and me with a tamal party. There, at my mom's casita in El Salvador, everyone came together. They chatted and laughed and threw shade at one another (most of the time jokingly). I will never forget what it felt like to be an adolescent hanging around such a huge tamalada. I had never seen so many señoras making tamales before then, or since.

That was also the first time in my life I ever ate a Salvadorian tamal and it was life-changing. It was gooey, soft, warm, and tasty. So fresh. Up until then, I had only eaten Mexican tamales from Sonora. In my teenage ignorance, I assumed those were the only kind of tamales that existed. (Good news: I have tasted many other tamales from different regions of Latin America since then!)

I wish I had paid more attention that day so I could have learned the recipe! But, as a teenager, cooking did not interest me. It was not until my adult years that I became interested in learning how to make Salvi tamales. Thankfully, after a lot of questions asked over the span of many Christmas holidays spent together, I learned a thing or two from my suegra.

Special shoutout to my suegra, because she and I made Salvi tamales for the photography in this book. We ended up with so many, that we gave them away to family and friends. Once she tasted them, my mom called me to sing my suegra's praises: "Wow, mija," she said. "These are the best Salvadorian tamales I have ever tasted!" I eagerly agreed.

Are you excited? Let's get to this recipe and go through the steps together!

With tamales, it is so hard to come up with precise measurements. My suegra and I racked our mind with how to come up with the right measurements as we tested this recipe. At the end of the day, I realized that some of the best señora cooking really does come from eyeballing the ingredients. And when it comes to tamales, you can expect to make too much. That's the beauty of tamales! You have enough to feed your entire clan, say, around the holidays, and enough to give away to loved ones as well.

LONG
You will be in the kitchen all day, but it's worth it!

DIFFICULTY
One of the ultimate señora-level dishes. Your tías will be saying that you're ready to get married!

SERVES
A LOT

Ingredients:

- Banana leaves, several
- 2 cans of garbanzo beans
- 1 jar of green olives
- Tomatoes, several to make a salsa
- 2 to 4 garlic cloves
- 2 whole onions
- 1 pinch of cumin
- Pumpkin seeds, about a handful
- 1 laurel leaf
- Sesame seeds, about a tablespoon
- Salt, al gusto
- Maseca, enough to make the masa (You will be adding it gradually to the masa)
- Olive oil, enough to mix into the masa to reach the desired consistency (You will be adding it gradually to the masa)
- Knorr chicken seasoning, al gusto
- Whole chicken or 2 large chicken breasts with bones
- Potatoes, about 6
- 1 celery stalk
- 1 bell pepper, optional

Directions:

PREP WORK

- Rinse the whole chicken and cut it into fourths. (You can also use chicken breasts with rib bones.)
- In a pot of boiling water, cook the whole chicken with tomato, garlic, celery, half an onion and Knorr chicken seasoning for about 20 minutes. Once cooked, set aside.
- While you allow the chicken to cook and cool, peel each garbanzo bean. Rinse.
- Peel the potatoes and cut them into strips. Put the potato strips in cool water so that they do not brown.
- Shred the cooled chicken.

MAKE THE SALSA

- On a comal, toast tomatoes, garlic, and remaining onion. You can also add a bell pepper. Once they have a beautiful and even golden color, you can set them to the side.
- Next, toast the sesame seeds, peppercorns, cumin, laurel leaf, and california pepper.
- Put all the toasted ingredients into a blender and blend until smooth. This is your salsa.
- Run the salsa through a strainer.
- In a separate bowl, get a tiny bit of salsa and mix with a bit of Maseca, run that through a strainer too and into the larger salsa mix. This allows for the salsa to thicken ever so slightly. If it is too runny, it will leak through the tamales.
- Put the salsa in a pot over medium heat, stirring constantly. You will see the salsa begin to thicken up. Turn off the flame and set the salsa to the side.

MAKE THE MASA

- In a large pot, mix the Maseca with olive oil and chicken broth to make the masa. It will have a liquid texture at this stage.
- Optional: Sift the Maseca through a strainer as you put it into your pot.
- Cook the masa in a large pot on medium heat. This step is necessary to thicken up the masa and achieve the rich texture we want for the tamales.
- Bring the masa to a boil. Stir constantly. (Stir like you have never stirred before! Stirring is imperative here both to create the desired texture and to avoid sticking to the edges.)
- You may need to add more oil and more water as you go in order to reach the desired texture for the masa.
- Give the masa a taste test and add salt or Knorr chicken-flavored seasoning if needed. We want a rich and savory masa.

- Keep stirring. You will see that, amazingly, the masa will go from being runny and watery to thicker, like horchata, then to a consistency of mashed potatoes, and, finally, to the thick texture that you want! The final texture will be almost like frosting.
- You will know the masa is ready with this test which my suegra's mother (who is no longer with us) shared with her: put a spoonful in the middle of a banana leaf and fold in half. If the masa sticks, add more oil and keep stirring. If the masa does not stick and glides easily on the banana leaf, then you are good to go.
- Once ready, set the masa aside to cool.

ASSEMBLE THE TAMALES

- Spread the masa across a banana leaf, place the shredded chicken, olive, garbanzo bean, and potato, and cover with a spoonful of sauce.
- Fold over the banana leaf tightly and wrap with foil.
- Pinch the edges to avoid masa from seeping out of the sides.
- Steam for about two hours in your designated tamal pot. You will know they are ready when the leaves are dark green and the potato is cooked and gets a soft texture.

¡Buen provecho!

TAMALES MEXICANOS DE SONORA

I could not write this particular book without including these tamales. First off, as I told you before, this book is all about honoring my culture through food, and who are the keepers of the recipes that make our culture so unique? Pues las doñas, of course! Your mom, tías, abuelitas, primas, sisters, cuñadas, nueras, suegras, and comadres. And nothing compares to the congregation of doñitas at a tamalada, aka a tamal-making party.

It's so much more than food: the chisme, the sass, the multitasking, the shade, the teamwork, the cooperation, and the storytelling are what make a tamalada, well, a real tamalada. Every mujer at a tamalada brings with her generations of cultural and family history. Don't you think the spirits of those matriarchs who are no longer with us hover around us, whispering in our ear, "add a pinch of this or that?" Or perhaps they are just watching proudly. Then you have the dons' help too. Maybe they have to stir the masa or carry the heavy pots from one table to another.

Every year on Christmas Eve, my family eats Mexican tamales from Sonora, and then on Christmas Day we reheat them on the comal. Growing up, we would make them in the kitchen at home where we had our own assembly line. As a little girl, I was in charge of putting an olive in every tamal. It helped me feel included and useful. As a teenager, I thought I was too cool for tamal parties.

I hosted my first tamalada last holiday season in my own kitchen. I was only a few weeks pregnant and my mom and I alone made all the tamales together. (She said I was slowing her down. Burn!) El Willy was out doing some last-minute Christmas shopping and Monchi was helping my mom and I carry heavy pots from one table to another. Monchi happily joked that next Christmas season I would be making tamales with a baby on my lap. Perhaps he would suck on an olive while I did my own part in the assembly line.

There I was, making a tamal recipe from Sonora that was passed down from my Nana Lupita (my great-grandma who I had the privilege of knowing until I was about ten years old) to my Nana Isabel to my mom, her nuera. It hit me that my mom and I, the two of us, were making the recipe of the matriarchs of my past, while the future generation grew in my belly. It was surreal. At that moment, this special recipe made me think of five generations of family. I will cherish the memory of that feeling forever. I cannot bite into a tamal without thinking of the past, present, and future all at once.

LONG
Get ready to be in the kitchen all day with your comadres!

DIFFICULTY
The ultimate señora level of cooking

SERVES

24 tamales
if you need more, simply increase the ingredients

Ingredients:

For the masa
- 1 cup of olive oil
- 3 cups of Maseca
- 2 cups of water
- 1 tablespoon Knorr beef-flavored seasoning

For the carne con chile filling
- 1 lb of chuck meat
- 6 guajillo chiles
- 6 California chiles
- 3 laurel leaves
- 1/2 of a red onion
- 3 jalapeños
- 3 roma tomatoes
- 3 garlic cloves
- 1 teaspoon of black peppercorns
- Salt, al gusto
- 1 can green olives, drained and rinsed
- 1/2 stick of organic grass-fed butter
- Mrs. Dash seasoning, al gusto
- 1 tablespoon Knorr beef-flavored seasoning

Directions:

COOK THE MEAT

- In a crockpot, slow cook the meat overnight (the night before your tamalada). Add the following seasonings: black peppercorns, salt, Mrs. Dash Seasoning, and the laurel leaves.
- Note: If you do not have a crock pot, you can also cook this meat in a large pot on simmer for about 3 hours.
- Once cooked, remove the meat from the pot and allow it to cool. Once cool, shred the cooked meat and set to the side. (Remove the laurel leaves). Save the broth, and set it aside.

PREPARE THE CHILE SAUCE

- Wash the vegetables.
- Remove seeds and stems from chiles.
- On a pan, on low heat, place the California pepper and guajillo peppers for a few minutes. You will know they are ready when they have a beautiful and even toasted color. (Gently toast the ingredients. If the chiles burn, it can give the sauce a bitter taste.)
- Put the toasted chiles in a glass bowl of hot water to soften them. Cover for 10 minutes.
- While the chiles rest in the hot water, put the tomatoes, garlic, onion and jalapeños on the pan. You want to chargrill these until they have a beautiful, even, toasted color. (Similar to how we toasted tomatoes and chiles in our salsa section.)
- Now, remove the chiles from the water and put them into a blender. Add the rest of the chargrilled ingredients to the blender as well.
- Add a pinch of oregano and 1 cup of the broth (leftover from the cooked meat) to the blender.
- Blend all the ingredients until smooth. We want a beautiful saucy texture here! (If your blender is not giving you the smoothest texture that is required for the sauce, run the blended sauce through a colander once.)
- Next, in a pan, vamos a guisar the sauce we just made. Prepare the pan on medium to low heat and melt half a stick of organic grass-fed butter to prevent sticking.
- Once the pan is evenly coated with the butter, add the sauce, a tablespoon of Knorr beef seasoning, and a pinch of salt.
- Stir constantly, until the sauce begins to bubble. Once it bubbles, fold in the shredded beef and drained olives.

If you stop here, you can enjoy an amazing Sonora style carne con chile. It tastes amazing with some buttery, paper-thin flour tortillas! This is one of my favorite foods.

- Allow the carne con chile to cool before preparing your tamales.
- As you wait for the meat to cool, prepare the masa and soak some corn husks in warm water.

MAKE THE MASA

- In a large bowl, add the Maseca. Sift through the dry Maseca with your fingers.
- Add salt and Knorr seasoning. Mix in well.
- Slowly add one cup of olive oil and mix in with your hands.
- Add water until you reach your desired texture: a gooey masa that can easily be spread but is not runny. Be slow and intentional here. You may find yourself needing a little more Maseca or a little extra water.

ASSEMBLE THE TAMALES

- With a rubber spatula, evenly spread the masa across the corn husk. (Be sure to always put the masa on the smoother side of the corn husk.)
- Add some of the carne con chile.
- Make sure to include the olive!
- Fold over the tamal.
- Place them in your designated tamal pot, fold-side down and open-side up.
- Steam in your designated tamal pot for about two hours.

¡Buen provecho!

A FINAL NOTE

During my pregnancy, I was subject to a bit of bed rest, which allowed me to slow down and really focus on writing this book, as I found myself having more free time than usual. The more progress I made, the more excited I became. I considered my son's due date to be my deadline to complete this book. Therefore, you can say that my son has been my biggest motivator since before he was even born.

My son was my biggest motivator and my family members were my biggest supporters: my husband, father, suegra, cuñadas, and, of course, my mother. I cannot tell you how many times Mama Rose and I sat down together to write out recipes or how difficult it was to come up with precise measurements. Every time I tried to ask my mom about a specific measurement she would answer "Ya sabes, un poco." After all, we Latinas are used to cooking by eyeballing ingredients and following our intuition. And it works every time!

Nonetheless, we moved forward with writing out recipes and testing the specific measurements. As my mother and I made progress, my belly grew, and so did our mother-daughter bond, which became stronger than ever.

I self-published this book because it is so personal to me. It was important to me to be involved in every step of the way. In the process, I named my publishing company Rosette Publications. It is a combination of my mom's name and my name. My goal was to portray our special connection.

I was named after Saint Bernadette of Lourdes, from France, who saw the Virgin Mary eighteen times. The first time she saw her was on February 11, 1858. My mother, Rose, was born on February 11, 1958. My mom felt a special connection to Saint Bernadette's story and the lessons her story offered. Therefore, Mama Rose promised the Virgin Mary she would, one day, name her daughter Bernadette.

I am the youngest of five children. I have two brothers and two sisters. Each one of us has a special story for how our names were chosen. For instance, at the excitement of my oldest sister, my mother named her after herself. My other sister, who is in the middle, was named after my grandmothers, at my father's request.

When my mom was pregnant with me, her fifth and last child, she prayed for a girl, so that she could keep her promise to la Virgencita. But I think I've been a jokester since conception because at every ultrasound, I hid. I crossed my legs, turned my back to the camera, you get the idea. The whole pregnancy, my parents wanted to know what they were having, but it was a surprise until I was born.

In the meantime, people came to their own conclusions. For instance, my father and his family were convinced I was a boy. They even referred to me as "junior" as I gestated in my mother's belly. My mom had a hunch that I was a girl (and hoped I was, due to her promise to la Virgencita). Mama tells me that she knew I would be her last child, and, therefore, the urgency to keep her promise persisted in her heart.

The Universe sent her signs that her hunch was spot on. One day, during her pregnancy, my mother shopped for groceries at a local market. At checkout, she noticed the cashier's name tag: Bernadette. At that time, Mama Rose had never met anyone named Bernadette in her thirty years of life! Yet suddenly, here she was seeing the name right before her eyes. My mother smiled and took it as a sign that perhaps she would be able to keep her promise after all.

The story of my name is something my mom lovingly shares with me often, and now I am so happy to share it with you. As you read through the recipes and stories of Herencia, I hope you can think fondly of the special bond that you may have with your own relatives, and how you have shown each other love through food. Here's to celebrating our connection to our ancestors and culture through food.

¡Buen provecho!

INDEX

Made in the USA
Monee, IL
29 November 2020